NEW PENGUIN SHAKESPEARE

GENERAL EDITOR: T. J. B. SPENCER

ASSOCIATE EDITOR: STANLEY WELLS

WILLIAM SHAKESPEARE

*

PERICLES
PRINCE OF TYRE

EDITED BY
PHILIP EDWARDS

PENGUIN BOOKS

Penguin Books Ltd, Harmondsworth, Middlesex, England
Penguin Books, 625 Madison Avenue, New York, New York 10022, U.S.A.
Penguin Books Australia Ltd, Ringwood, Victoria, Australia
Penguin Books Canada Ltd, 2801 John Street, Markham, Ontario, Canada L3R 1B4
Penguin Books (N.Z.) Ltd, 182–190 Wairau Road, Auckland 10, New Zealand

—

This edition first published in Penguin Books 1976
Reprinted 1981

—

This edition copyright © Penguin Books, 1976
Introduction and notes copyright © Philip Edwards, 1976
All rights reserved

—

Made and printed in Great Britain
by Richard Clay (The Chaucer Press) Ltd,
Bungay, Suffolk
Set in Monotype Ehrhardt

CONTENTS

MAP TO ILLUSTRATE THE WANDERINGS OF
PERICLES   6

INTRODUCTION   7

FURTHER READING   43

PERICLES, PRINCE OF TYRE   45

COMMENTARY   139

AN ACCOUNT OF THE TEXT   193

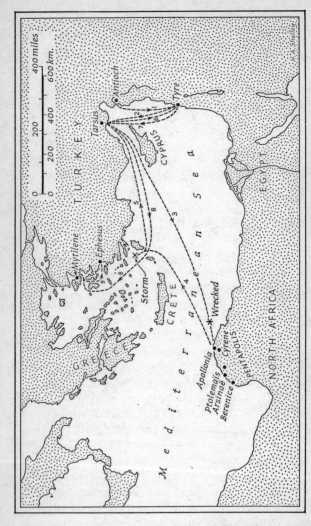

Map to illustrate the wanderings of Pericles (*see the Commentary to* III.1.76)

INTRODUCTION

In 1608 *Pericles, Prince of Tyre* was being performed with great success by Shakespeare's company, the King's Men, at the Globe Theatre. An indication of its popularity is that the Venetian ambassador paid over twenty crowns for a special performance, to which he took the French ambassador and his wife and a visitor from Florence. Unhappily the authentic text of this play has not come down to us, and part of the reason why we have to put up with a debased text is the very popularity of the play. It was not the habit of the King's Men, or other companies, to lose their sole rights in plays by publishing them to the world. But there was a strong demand for the printed texts of plays – from those who had seen a play, from those who had not, and from actors who wanted to cash in on a popular play by performing it themselves. For this reason there was a steady supply of pirated plays, unauthorized versions put together in one way or another. Shakespeare had for a long time suffered from the pirates, and inauthentic texts, now known as 'bad quartos', had been published of several of his plays, including *Romeo and Juliet*, *Henry V*, and *Hamlet*. The first attempt to exploit the popularity of *Pericles* was a harmless enough publication, a prose narrative by George Wilkins called *The Painful Adventures of Pericles, Prince of Tyre*, claiming to be 'the true history of the play of *Pericles*', as it had been 'by the King's Majesty's Players excellently presented'. This was in 1608. The next year saw a publication in play form. 'The late and much admired play' they called it on the title-page, and added 'By William Shakespeare'. This Quarto, in which there are probably not five consecutive genuine lines, was at once used by players in Yorkshire (who also acted *King Lear* from a seemingly unauthorized printed version). There was no attempt by the King's Men to replace this text by the genuine one (as the pirated version of *Hamlet* had been replaced). They continued to act their play, and the publishers continued to reprint the bad text. (Six editions had appeared by 1635.) One wonders whether at one of their revivals of the play the King's Men discovered that the manuscript was missing and were forced back on the pirated version. For whatever reason, the only text of *Pericles* which we have to this day is the poor text originally published in 1609.

When, therefore, we talk about *Pericles* as it was acted by Shakespeare's company in its heyday, we are talking about a hidden play, a play concealed from us by a text full of confusion and with a clumsiness and poverty of language unrivalled in the Shakespeare canon. Yet, encrusted and deformed though it is, this hidden play reveals itself in glimpses as a work of remarkable beauty and power. Much credit must be given to the English stage, which in successive productions after the Second World War at Birmingham, Stratford-upon-Avon, and elsewhere demonstrated that there was an unusual magic in the work. It happened, as it often happens with Ibsen or Greek drama in English, that stage action was somehow able to re-create the true effectiveness of scenes which an impoverished language quite spoils for a reader.

*

In *Pericles*, it would seem that a great deal of subtlety and care went into giving the impression of a work of artless simplicity, even naivety. The play is based on the very ancient tale of Apollonius of Tyre, a Greek romance which was told and retold throughout Europe for a thousand years. In England, John Gower gave a rendering of it in his *Confessio Amantis* in the late fourteenth century, and another version, translated by Laurence Twine in 1576, had been reissued in 1607 (*The Pattern of Painful Adventures*). That the story was honoured by time and had given pleasure not only to the people at their holidays and festivals but also to aristocratic readers is insisted on in the opening lines of the prologue of the play. The presenter, the medieval poet Gower, who is brought back from the dead to retell the tale, himself emphasizes the antiquity of the story. Gower as presenter seems to have impressed the audience at the Globe. The title-page of Wilkins's narrative has a woodcut not of Pericles or Marina but of Gower, and it speaks of the play 'as it was lately presented by the worthy and ancient poet John Gower'. And Wilkins concludes a prefatory note with the words: 'Only entreating the reader to receive this history in the same manner as it was under the habit of ancient Gower, the famous English poet, by the King's Majesty's Players excellently presented.'

Those who pirated the text seem to have had difficulty not only with the quaint archaism of the language given to Gower but also with the sophistication of his role as presenter, and his 'choruses' are full of faults. He is *presenting* the story, an ancient narrative, a romance covering a lifetime, full of marvels and miracles, strokes of good and bad fortune, kindness and malevolence, providential rescues, love, marriage, birth, and death, visiting in its course seas and cities all over the Mediterranean. This kind of romance had been popular on the English stage thirty years earlier, embarrassing learned men like Sir Philip Sidney, who protested against such childishness in his *Apology for Poetry*. It comes forward now in *Pericles* in all consciousness of itself and perhaps with some defiance. Gower lets us watch him selecting those parts of his story best suited for narration, those which can be enacted in mime or dumb show, and those which can be most effectively shown by performed action. Gower gets rid of illusion and calls attention to the play as a fabrication. The reality of the story is to be created by his skill as a narrator and the skill of the actors who appear at his command, coupled with the willing engagement of the audience's imagination. He looks about him – 'This Antioch, then' – and proceeds with his story until he gets to 'So for her many a wight did die', when he points to a semblance of severed heads above the stage, 'As yon grim looks do testify'. He then turns to leave the stage, giving the story over to the actors who are now appearing; they 'best can justify' it – that is, make it appear true. In the chorus which begins Act III, having narrated the story of the marriage of Pericles and Thaisa, and having brought on the actors for a dumb show of the news from Tyre, Gower proceeds with his story and ends thus:

> *And what ensues in this fell storm*
> *Shall for itself itself perform.*
> *I nill relate, action may*
> *Conveniently the rest convey....*

And then, as he withdraws,

> *In your imagination hold*
> *This stage the ship, upon whose deck*
> *The sea-tossed Pericles appears....*

In Act IV, scene 4, Gower points out as he has done before how imagination going along with his narrative can consume time and banish space. He says he stands 'i'th'gaps' to convey 'The stages of our story'. As the actors depart after yet another mime, this time the dumb show in which Pericles is acquainted with the death of his daughter by the hypocrites Cleon and Dionyza, Gower contrasts the acting of an untruth by Cleon and Dionyza with the acting of true grief by the *actor* taking the part of Pericles (IV.4.24). This is a striking pointer to the play's demand to be accepted as an acted fiction.

It would be a great mistake to see Gower's manipulation of his three kinds of exposition (narrative, mime, and full stage action) as a reflection of the play's simple-mindedness. The effect indeed is of something primitive and quaint, but that effect must have been seriously intended. The interchange of devices seems to be an attempt to deepen the power of romance by giving it the vividness of performance without losing the indispensable relaxed air of a story-telling which takes a long time and treats of many years. An atavism of technique casts over the whole the sentimental glow of times past so important for the nostalgic Elizabethans. The more primitive the dumb shows seem, the more they serve the purpose of a play which is determined to be an antique. Medievalism is much more noticeable in the play than it is in the genuine medieval version which the real John Gower told in his *Confessio Amantis*. The slow-moving pageantry of the parade of the knights at Pentapolis, each one in full armour with his page carrying an emblematic shield, and the jousting which follows are inventions of the dramatist. But the story as a whole is not placed within the age of chivalry. The worship of Diana at Ephesus at the end of the play and the founding of Antioch at the beginning contrast strikingly with the medieval note and help to give the feeling of all-time and no-time which we assume was intended.

From what has already been said, it will be seen that much importance is given in *Pericles* to the fact of a stage which, as Gower's words guide the imagination of the audience, is transformed into a succession of different, widely-separated places. *Pericles* insists on its locations, insists that they are physically there while agreeing with us that they are not. It is not wrong to think of the play as a series of composed spectacles, almost tableaux, each in its given and proper place. We see the riddle solved below the bloody battlements of Antioch; the starving inhabitants of Tarsus grouped round their ruler and his wife; the fishermen casting their nets from the shore; the procession of the knights, the banquet and the dance at Pentapolis; Pericles with the infant Marina on the deck of the storm-tossed ship; the opening of the coffin at Ephesus; Marina on the sea-shore at Tarsus; Marina and the bawds in the brothel at Mytilene; the temple of Diana with her priestesses ranged before it at Ephesus. Particularly interesting in this demand that we see the stage both as a stage and as another place is the repeated use which seems to have been made of the curtained recess in the rear wall of the stage (what used to be called the inner stage). This is first used when Lychorida draws back the curtains to show Pericles the dead body of Thaisa (III.1.55); it is used again for the tomb of Marina at Tarsus in the dumb show in Act IV, scene 4; and finally it is used to reveal the inert figure of Pericles himself in the harbour at Mytilene (V.1.32). Wife, daughter, husband; each, in a sense, shown for dead in that curtained space, and each later made alive. The same curtained recess is made to travel widely in place and function but the unity of its uses is proclaimed by its being after all the same curtained recess.

There is, then, an emphasis in the scenes of *Pericles* on physical place, on a formality in grouping, and a certain ceremony in the action. To these we must add music as a presence in the play. There is music for the entrance of Antiochus's daughter in the first scene, music for the dance at Pentapolis (II.3), music for the revival of Thaisa (III.2.87–90), the song which Marina sings to arouse Pericles (V.1.78), and the 'music of the spheres' announcing the vision of Diana at the end of the play. Music, ceremony, grouping, location: the mind of the audience is approached physically; the words of the actors are given a kind of visual, aural, tactile frame. This is as it should be when enactment on a stage is offered as a deliberate alternative to the more mental or subjective creation of a story told only by a narrator. *Pericles* is a statuesque sort of play, and its scenes remain strongly in the mind as sculpted groups.

*

The attempt to bring to life old-world romance and pageantry did not succeed with everyone. Ben Jonson called *Pericles* 'a mouldy tale'; he and others seem to have been disgusted by the popularity of this simple thing. It is in its courting the scorn of the sophisticated that I find a note of defiance in *Pericles*. In that all-important opening chorus, Gower bows to the condescension of modernity:

> *If you, born in these latter times*
> *When wit's more ripe, accept my rhymes,*
> *And that to hear an old man sing*
> *May to your wishes pleasure bring. . . .*

There may be a challenge in the phrase 'When wit's more ripe'. *Pericles* suggests that in the unrealistic adventures of romance, the journeyings, the shipwrecks, the restoring of the dead, uniting of the sundered, there can be found images of human life as compelling as in the severer naturalism of satirical comedy or the intenser articulation of conflict and catastrophe in tragedy. The play is quite ridiculous seen from any standard of probability or the expectations of ordinary life. Its unlifelikeness is not only in its coincidences and marvels, like the 'saving' of Marina by the pirates, or her being brought face to face with her father, but in the extreme simplification of character and of human encounter. The good are good and the bad are bad. Changes of moral state (Dionyza, Lysimachus, Boult) are as uncomplicated and unconvincing as the moral states themselves.

The striking lack of connexion between character, deed, and event in *Pericles* is perhaps less an offence against life than against art. Many commentators, conditioned to find in drama a full relationship between what people are and what they do and what happens to them, have tried to create a moral meaning for *Pericles* by relating the hero's sufferings and rewards to his sins and his virtues. Although these patterns are not absent from the play, they cannot be made to account for its structure. *Pericles* is a string of adventures, mostly misfortunes, ending in a climax of happiness. It does not have an inevitable and inexorable movement which can only be explained in the light of the hero's temperament and deeds. When he was told that *The Ancient Mariner* was improbable and had no moral, Coleridge agreed about the improbability but thought it a fault of his poem that the moral sentiment obtruded so openly as a principle or cause of action in a work of such pure imagination. 'It ought to have had no more moral than the Arabian Nights' tale of the merchant's sitting down to eat dates by the side of a well, and throwing the shells aside, and lo! a genie starts up, and says he *must* kill the aforesaid merchant, *because* one of the date shells had, it seems, put out the eye of the genie's son' (*Table Talk*, 31 May 1830). *Pericles*, like *The Ancient Mariner* a tale of voyaging and marvels which tempts us to see many kinds of spiritual significance in its incidents, achieves that freedom from the moral link of deed and suffering which Coleridge desired. For Dionyza to start up and say she *must* kill Marina *because* her beauty and accomplishments make her overshadow her own daughter is a grim refinement of the logic of the genie, whose son had in fact lost an eye. *Pericles* is a profoundly moral work, and may well seem too one-sided in its views on culpability and responsibility, but it does not obtrude its moral views as principles or causes of the action. To account for Pericles' sufferings in terms of his rashness in casting Thaisa to the waves or of his neglect in leaving Marina to be brought up by Dionyza is quite to miss the mark.

A good Renaissance writer used romance with full consciousness of the extravagance and absurdity of its conventions. Its quests, its infatuations, its coincidences, its simplification of people and moral issues and conflicts, were employed not because the writer thought life was like that but because he knew it was not. It was the freedom from verisimilitude that attracted the writer. No doubt in its fondness for romance the Renaissance was looking for its own lost innocence, but the main reason why the simple and clear-cut issues of romance were so tempting was that they provided a hospitality to moral meaning which a greater naturalism might not be able to offer. Ideas of chastity, or nobility, or courage, images of bereavement and affection, misery and happiness, endurance and despair, oppositions of good and evil, could easily and strikingly be supplied by the world of romance. Also, romance is built of elements which are readily charged with universal or spiritual meanings. Battles with giants, discovery of lost children, quests through forests, voyages and shipwrecks; all these are readily turned to symbolic use or allegory. Erich Auerbach, in Chapter 6 of his famous book *Mimesis* (1946), was highly critical of romance because of the political and practical emptiness of its adventures. But when a journey is emptied of an immediate practical purposefulness it can become big with symbolic possibilities.

So the author of *Pericles* perhaps thought it worth risking Ben Jonson's scowl. A number of things are made possible by the materials and conventions of romance. One major triumph is the sense of the passage of a lifetime. Pericles, the ardent young man seeking a bride in the first scene, is by the end of the play the father in middle life, who has undergone so much experience and suffering, giving away his daughter in marriage. The action in fact covers little more than fifteen years, but the apparent stretch of time is expanded by the inclusion of marriage, birth, and death within the action, and by the unkempt locks and beard (fourteen years' growth) which the actor of Pericles is required to have in the final scenes. Gower's insistence on the change of place and the passage of time does much to remove any sense of absurdity in the compression of so many years into two hours. Our sense of a lifetime's experience is enhanced by the very discontinuity of the action (a discontinuity which is emphasized by the rapid alterations of place). *Pericles* is built of a series of concentrated 'moments'. Though they have a before and after, these moments are unusually self-contained. Because cause and effect are not very important, all the concentration goes on to the emotions of the moment. Scenes are searched for their own value and not for what they may lead to. The shock of discovering incest at Antioch, the grief at the death of Thaisa in childbirth, the wonder of seeing Thaisa brought back to life, the victory of Marina over Boult, these are the things which are held in the camera. Each scene is prefaced by a gigantic *if*. '*If* a wife had been buried at sea, but she was not really dead, and she was washed up on a shore where there lived a famous healer, *then* these would be our emotions as she was brought back to life.' Comparatively isolated scenes, each generating its own emotions, are accumulated to build an arch of time which spans many years.

In building this arch, the play suggests the passage not only of individual lifetimes but also of human life itself, as a number of commentators, first and chief among them G. Wilson Knight, have shown. In creating this effect, that *sine qua non* of romance the sea is all-important. We are never far from the sea in *Pericles*, and it needs no effort on our part to look on it as the sea of life, the flow of unaccountable circumstances in which we drift. Twice the sea wrecks Pericles. Out of the first wreck comes the kindness of the fishermen and the winning of Thaisa. The second shipwreck leads to the loss of Thaisa and eventually to the malevolence of the brothel. Pericles' ships bring corn to starving Tarsus. Marina, the 'fresh new seafarer', walks on the strand at Tarsus and is swept away from death by pirates who take her over the sea to Mytilene. And it is in a ship floating in harbour that Marina, born at sea, meets her father again and gives him back the will to live. It is the sea which casts up the chest with Thaisa in. The sea threatens and comforts, destroys and rebuilds, separates and unites.

*

In a play which builds a lifetime out of a multiplicity of incidents, the real continuity is in the development of relationships. In spite of all its adventures, in spite of the importance of Pericles being a prince with a country and its people to govern, the play is chiefly concerned with the quadruple relationship of husband, wife, daughter, and daughter's suitor. The link between father and daughter receives the strongest lighting.

Three times the play presents these relationships to us. At the opening, we have Antiochus as father, his daughter acting as both daughter and wife, and Pericles as the suitor. In the middle of the play, Simonides is the father, Thaisa the daughter, and Pericles is again the suitor. At the end of the play, Pericles is the father, Thaisa the wife, Marina the daughter, and Lysimachus the suitor. In the different relationships shown in each group lies most of the play's meaning. The contrasts were probably made sharper in early performances by doubling Antiochus with Simonides (and perhaps Lysimachus), and Antiochus's daughter with Thaisa.

Antiochus and his nameless daughter are bound together in incestuous lust, an all-excluding link which is death to those who try to break it. Wilson Knight writes well in *The Crown of Life* of the way Pericles approaches the daughter, this 'dazzling creature', his extravagant praise having in it 'something a trifle feverish; it is the result more of fascination, almost lust, than love.' He notes how Pericles sanctifies his frank desire as god-implanted:

> You gods . . .
> That have inflamed desire in my breast
> To taste the fruit of yon celestial tree
> Or die in the adventure, be my helps . . .

But this 'golden fruit', as her father calls it, is infernal, not celestial. The desire is infected and the object is corrupt.

Antiochus's riddle contains a grim couplet showing all relationship confounded:

> *He's father, son, and husband mild;*
> *I mother, wife, and yet his child.*   I.1.69–70

From this confusion, and the threat of death, Pericles escapes. His own chosen path led him to a place of corruption and murder; now the accident of shipwreck brings him to the court of Simonides where he finds his bride. At Pentapolis, there is a very simple triangle. There is Simonides the father, jovial, peremptory, loving his innocent deceptions, wishing his daughter to have her own will in marriage and, fortunately, thoroughly approving of her choice; there is Thaisa, young and beautiful, who falls in love at first sight with the mysterious stranger; and there is Pericles himself, winning the contest and his bride entirely by his personality and ability, being unknown and deprived of all his possessions, the 'mean knight' in rusty armour. This innocent little picture of father, daughter, and suitor is put there in all its ingenuousness, and in the theatre it produces the pleasure appropriate to it. In the strong chiaroscuro of this play it stands against the darkness of evil in Antiochus and the very different darkness of the bereavement at sea which follows.

Pericles loses his wife and then, as she grows to womanhood, his daughter. He continues to live, but he is dead to the world. The play turns its attention to Marina. She is introduced by Gower as a fairy-tale princess, all beauty and accomplishments, challenged by the murderous envy of a foster-mother. Like her father, she survives an attempt to kill her, but the cost of her escape is to be sold to the Mytilene brothel. Here she meets her great ordeal, the test of the quality of her being, the test which heroes of romance all must undergo to prove themselves. In emerging triumphantly, she becomes a person who can charge others with new life.

Although the brothel incident is in the play's source, and although virgins courageously defending their honour are a very common theme in romance, it might seem in *Pericles* that the stark and deeply etched realism of the brothel makes it simply the wrong place for a creature of fairy tale like Marina; that Boult and Marina belong to two different conventions of art and that to mix them is to mix Walter Scott and William Burroughs, or Jane Austen and Zola. There *is* a mixture of genres, but it is a purposeful and important mingling. The brothel-keepers balance the fishermen of Act II (almost certainly the parts were doubled) as creatures from a more 'real' world than the world of the rest of the characters. As the fishermen represent the rough good-heartedness of the rural poor, the brothel people represent the corruption, disease, and cruelty of urban life. Figures of romance, the noble prince in the first place and the virgin princess in the second, are thrust among creatures of naturalism whom they thoroughly bewilder. The achievement of this perhaps risky juxtaposition of earth and air is that the audience is made aware that the dramatist knows of another world and they can see him testing the different valuations of experience contained within different conventions of art, testing ideals against knowledge. The divinity most frequently mentioned in *Pericles* is Diana, goddess of chastity. It is her temple in Ephesus to which Thaisa retires as a priestess; it is she who appears to Pericles in a vision and directs him to find his wife. When Marina, threatened by the assaults of the brothel's customers, swears to remain a virgin even if she has to kill herself, she calls on Diana to aid her purpose (IV.2.142). 'What have we to do with

20

Diana?' sneers the old mother-bawd. And that is just the question which the play poses. What *have* we to do with Diana, and such-like circus animals of old-fashioned romance?

To those who run the brothel, Marina's chastity is felt as more than a loss of trade. It is an offence against their values (IV.6.133–4). She will not 'go the way of woman-kind' as they see it. Boult is to rape her and 'make the rest malleable' not as a punishment and to make her fit for the trade only, but to reduce her to their level. Even before Marina enters the brothel, a tiny but brilliant comic exchange shows the Pander already ill at ease about the ethics of his profession (IV.2.10–37). The coming of Marina is like the arrival of an avenging angel they have half expected. 'She's born to undo us' (IV.6.146–7). Al-though the conversation of the two gentlemen converted by Marina (IV.5) is pure comedy ('Shall's go hear the vestals sing?'), there is no escaping the fact that it is part of what these great scenes in the brothel are presenting at a level deeper than the laughter and deeper than the literal sense: the idea of purification, the *possibility* of it in this climate of easy-going, casual sexual gratification.

The contest between Marina and Lysimachus is the hub of this matter, and in many ways the hub of the whole play. It is the greatest misfortune that what our text gives us looks like a clumsy abbreviation of the original ex-changes. Lysimachus, the governor of Mytilene, enters the brothel, disguising himself from the eyes of the people. He is well known to the three keepers and he cheerfully numbers himself among the house's 'resorters'. He is anxious that the girl he has should not be diseased, and his flippant reaction to the sight of Marina is 'Faith, she would serve after a long voyage at sea'. When they are alone, he chats to her with an off-hand condescension that shows no recognition of her as a person: 'Now, pretty one, how long have you been at this trade?' He is quite uninterested in her replies and says impatiently 'Come, bring me to some private place.' Marina rather briefly appeals to him and laments her misfortune. There is a strong possibility that the 1609 text at this point misrepresents Lysimachus's behaviour.

> *I did not think thou couldst have spoke so well,*
> *Ne'er dreamt thou couldst.*
> *Had I brought hither a corrupted mind,*
> *Thy speech had altered it. Hold, here's gold for thee....*
> *For me, be you thoughten*
> *That I came with no ill intent; for to me*
> *The very doors and windows savour vilely.*
>
> IV.6.99–102, 106–8

This moment is of great importance. The natural interpretation of Lysimachus's words is that he never had any designs on Marina and that his threatened assault was all a pretence. Is Lysimachus arranging an ordeal, like the Green Knight in the medieval poem, or is he a part of the ordeal? Is the encounter between Marina and Lysimachus an image of the purification of a man who sins through thoughtlessness, or a testing of Marina's virtue by a prince who has no thought of violating her? Either way, the brothel is Marina's ordeal; but is the climax of that ordeal real or faked?

The encounter is very differently dealt with in the prose narrative by George Wilkins, *The Painful Adventures of Pericles, Prince of Tyre*. In this curious work, Marina is given long speeches in which she attacks the dishonourableness of Lysimachus and pleads with him to spare her. Lysimachus, whose earlier behaviour has been more threatening, makes no claim that he has only been dissembling.

> ... he lift her up with his hands ... saying aside 'Now
> surely this is virtue's image, or rather virtue's self, sent
> down from heaven a while to reign on earth to teach us
> what we should be.... I hither came with thoughts
> intemperate, foul and deformed, the which your pains so
> well have laved that they are now white ... for my part,
> who hither came but to have paid the price, a piece of
> gold for your virginity, now give you twenty to relieve
> your honesty....'

It has more than once been persuasively argued that Wilkins's version represents an earlier stage of the play than that which is reported in the 1609 text. The argument is both linguistic and moral. It is linguistic in that Wilkins's prose, which clearly reveals fossils of blank verse, is not at all like the writing which the play exhibits at this point. It is moral in that (it is argued) the 1609 Quarto shows a development in the character of Lysimachus, an alteration to make him a prince more acceptable as the future husband of Marina; Wilkins therefore represents an unrevised and coarser concept of the part of Lysimachus. The linguistic argument can be discussed only in the context of Wilkins's style as a whole in his narrative, and is not, I think, decisive. The moral argument has to be faced. The objection to the theory of a revision is that, except for the inversion of two sentences, no revision of Lysimachus's role is perceptible in the Quarto. For Lysimachus to be changed into the stage-manager of the ordeal, two alterations would have been necessary. First, he should have been invested with the kind of dignity and awe which we associate with those grand deceivers the Duke in *Measure for Measure* and

Prospero in *The Tempest* – dignity and awe such as are given in this play to Cerimon. Secondly, the audience would have to be given some hint that Marina was in reality safe all the time. With these conditions, the subjection of Marina to the torment of this show of sexual bullying might be acceptable to an Elizabethan audience, even if not to us. Without these conditions, Lysimachus as 'tester' can only be seen as quite revoltingly callous and cruel, and the audience must be furious at the deception practised on *them*. These conditions are not met; in the Quarto there is no preparation for the semi-divine role of organizing a moral purgatory, and no notice of a deception is given to the audience. As has been seen, Lysimachus's entry is that of a well-known client of the brothel. Nor does the Quarto contain the word or action which must have followed a testing. Lysimachus offers no word of explanation to Marina, and makes no apology for the strain and distress he has subjected her to. It is noticeable that the modern theatre finds great difficulty in fitting those key words of Lysimachus, explaining that he 'came with no ill intent', into the staging of the scene. At Birmingham in 1954 the Repertory Theatre actually used a form of words taken from Wilkins indicating that Marina had converted Lysimachus. The Prospect Theatre Company in 1973 simply left the words out (and by thus further abbreviating an already truncated scene they quite bewildered their audience).

We meet fewer obstacles if we suppose that no revision took place in this scene, and that Wilkins and the Quarto are both writing up or trying to reassemble the same stage version of the encounter. Each report contains something the other has missed, but in the vital matter of the innocence or otherwise of Lysimachus's intentions, Wilkins must be right. It may be that, on the stage,

Lysimachus in his apology made a distinction between irresponsibility and evil intent, even that he denied a corruption of his mind while admitting a fault in his conduct. The reporter may have misunderstood his notes; or he too may have had a preference for a 'purer' husband for Marina.

The moral issue is not easy. If, as I have argued, the idea that Lysimachus never intended to have sexual relations with Marina is repugnant on the grounds that it involves a cruel deception of Marina and an irritating deception of the audience, we then have to meet the argument that it is repugnant that a prince who has sought his gratifications in such a horrible place as this brothel, and has there met and been shamed by Marina, should then be presented as a suitable husband for her. Yet Shakespeare thought Angelo a fit husband for Mariana, and Angelo's intentions against Isabella were worse than Lysimachus's against Marina. It is true that the crudeness of the Quarto in the last act does not help Lysimachus to appear as successfully in his role as princely suitor as he did in his role as flippant whoremonger. Much depends on the actor in a stage presentation, but the *idea* of the whoremonger becoming a bridegroom is surely not offensive. Marina's transformation of the man who casually sought her as a prostitute into a man who woos her for his wife, and her acceptance in marriage of the man whose sexual advances she spurned in the brothel, are her victory, a victory as important and as total as Lena's victory in Conrad's great story. It is not in the least a matter of Marina's being prepared to accept the embraces of Lysimachus once she has, like Richardson's Pamela, won the safeguard of the marriage-lines. The difference in the situation is not a promise of marriage but an attitude towards sexual relations. For Lysimachus, Marina was first simply an object to satisfy his sexual desire. Because of her response to him and the force of her very being, he recognizes her as a person and by that recognition is himself an altered being. The alteration shows not in the abandonment of his desire for her but in its transmutation, so that he seeks her love and not just her body. There is a similar though much less sharply presented alteration in Pericles. He pursued Antiochus's daughter with a kind of lust; he is not for that reason disqualified as the bridegroom of Thaisa. It is generous of Marina not to despise Lysimachus, but her acceptance of his love is a measure of the alteration of his nature which she has brought about, and such power as hers seems to me a main subject of the play. If we take it that Marina does not alter Lysimachus, because he never was an irresponsible sinner, we have taken much of the heart out of the play.

Marina emerges from the brothel after triumphing in a second encounter, this time with Boult, who tries to rape her. She confounds the brothel people and their values, bringing Diana into their astonished lives. With the new power which her successful endurance of her ordeal gives her, she is brought before Pericles, neither father nor daughter knowing the other. Even before he realizes who she is, she brings new life to him and makes his sufferings seem petty.

> *thou dost look*
> *Like Patience gazing on kings' graves and smiling*
> *Extremity out of act.*   V.1.137-9

The power of this scene in which Pericles discovers that this maid is in fact his supposedly-dead daughter is something which only the stage can convey. A reader gets a little of it. A summary provides nothing. Marina comes

back to life (or so it seems to Pericles) and thereby brings
him back to life. He awakens to such joy that he fears

> *Lest this great sea of joys rushing upon me*
> *O'erbear the shores of my mortality*
> *And drown me with their sweetness.*   V.1.193–5

Then he addresses her with the greatest lines which the
compilers of the text have preserved for us:

> *O, come hither,*
> *Thou that beget'st him that did thee beget;*
> *Thou that wast born at sea, buried at Tarsus,*
> *And found at sea again.*   V.1.195–8

With the line 'Thou that beget'st him that did thee
beget', it is scarcely possible not to think back to the
relationship between Antiochus and his daughter. The
figure of speech which Pericles uses equates the spiritual
renewal which Marina brings about in him with her
physical birth for which he was responsible. The figure of
speech was an ancient Christian paradox for the miracle of
God the father becoming the son of his virgin daughter.
In the play, father and daughter are bound in a reciprocal
bond of affection, each owing life to the other, each aware
of the need of the other. In Antioch, father and daughter
also confused their relationship, but the reciprocity of
their affection was in sexual need and the perversion of the
natural relationship. At the moment when Pericles and
Marina recover each other and acknowledge their depen-
dence on each other, Diana appears to Pericles and tells
him where his wife is to be found. The discovery of Thaisa
in Ephesus restores Pericles to his own marriage partner
and shows the absence of any taint of Antioch from his
relations with Marina, who in her turn takes the marriage
partner of her own generation, Lysimachus.

The play takes a view of chastity which is at the same time mystical, puritanical, and accommodating. In its view of virginity withstanding ordeal and evolving into a chastity which includes sexuality, it provides a link between Spenser's *The Faerie Queene* and Milton's *Comus*. (For Milton's knowledge of the play, see the Commentary to III.1.63.) It is as a virgin and to preserve her virginity that Marina fights off both the bawds and the clients in the brothel. Her virginity almost miraculously asserts its power. She is then free to create the two relationships which matter most in the play, the sexual relationship between wife and husband and the non-sexual relationship between daughter and father. Diana, the goddess of virginity, may in this play release her own priestess from her devotions and restore her to her husband. Thaisa says

> *If he be none of mine, my sanctity*
> *Will to my sense bend no licentious ear . . .*
>
> V.3.29–30

meaning that sanctity for her as for her daughter comprehends either celibacy, or sexuality in marriage. There is no conflict. If he is not her husband, she returns to the service of Diana.

What it seems *Pericles* tries to achieve is a vision (it is hardly anything else) of the sexual relationship contained within marriage, and of the generations joined by a link of affection even stronger and more spiritual than the relation of husband and wife, namely the relation of parent and child.

*

The concord of relationships at the end of *Pericles* is something which the characters do not so much achieve as reach, at the end of a long and difficult journey that had no destination. It is time to turn back to the sea, and to the difficult question how far *Pericles* is to be read as a spiritual journey, and how far the characters are under the direction of spiritual forces. 'The gods' are on everyone's lips in *Pericles*, appealed to for help or pointed to as the cause of what is happening. Many pagan gods are named: Lucina, Apollo, Juno, Priapus, Aesculapius, and, above all, Neptune and Diana. After Diana, goddess of chastity, the divinity who makes the strongest appearance in *Pericles* is Neptune, the sea-god, whom Pericles appeals to in the storm as 'The god of this great vast' (III.1.1; see also III Chorus 45). The final mention of Neptune in the play is important. The reunion between Marina and Pericles takes place in Pericles' ship in the harbour at Mytilene, where, Gower tells us, the 'annual feast' of 'God Neptune' is being celebrated by the town. The feast is mentioned a second time by Lysimachus (V.1.16). It seems that a point is being made when father and daughter are brought together in harbour, where after so much storm the sea is quiet, in a city where the power of the sea-god is being celebrated. Supernatural intervention follows when ¦Diana appears in a vision to direct Pericles to Ephesus. There, when he has found his wife, whom for years he had supposed to be dead, he tells her that he longs to know

> who to thank,
> Besides the gods, for this great miracle.

THAISA

> Lord Cerimon, my lord; this man
> Through whom the gods have shown their power; that can
> From first to last resolve you.

PERICLES   *Reverend sir,*

> The gods can have no mortal officer
> More like a god than you. Will you deliver
> How this dead queen re-lives?   V.3.57–64

29

It is worth noting that the revival of Thaisa by Cerimon was by natural and not supernatural means. Cerimon used his profound knowledge of nature to effect the cure of one who had not fully passed the boundary of death (III.2.30–37, 80–82). Of the knowledge of natural things which he has acquired, he says immortality attends it, 'Making a man a god' (III.2.30). Although the agency is human, the circumstances of the scene, with its music and poetry, suggest a near-miracle, bringing to the hushed stage and audience a hint of the mystery of divine strength entering a chosen human vessel.

In the last act, then, by the use of Neptune, Diana, and Cerimon, the audience is strongly encouraged to agree with the view of the characters – who all along have seen themselves as subject to fortune and the gods – that the happy outcome of all their adventures is due to divine providence. But it must be said that in the play taken as a whole divine guidance and direction seem fitful and inconstant. To see the entire play as a representation of a pattern of perceived and understood providence would be as wrong as to see it as a kind of *Pilgrim's Progress* in which the characters persevere towards a known goal of redemption and salvation. There is no pattern, either of providence or of redemption. The play is about people who suffer unaccountable misfortunes and gain equally unaccountable good fortune. At all times, these people retain the conviction that, although its course and purposes are inscrutable, providence must exist. The happy outcome supports that conviction. More strongly even than this, the sense of a divine presence in the world is suggested by the mysterious human power of Marina and Cerimon. Men and women exist who in the depth of their learning or in the strength of their innocence have the power to change others, to revive and re-create them, and this power suggests divine help. In its treatment of providence and of the presence of divine strength in people, the play tends to affirm both the certainty that the supernatural is active on earth, and also the complete mystery of its ways.

In the end, the simplicity of the relationships in *Pericles*, the unlikelihood of the events, the lack of cause-and-effect in the plot, make the play a presentation of images which, while individually they expand into wide and general meanings, yet as a whole sequence withdraw from asserting how things run in this world. We are offered ideas or propositions about love and suffering and chastity, and the relation of them to a divine will, but we are not offered a clue to any meaning lying in the progression of events. The sea, therefore, remains a mystery. Neptune and Aeolus, the waves and the wind, are a great force and our lives are in their hands. We have the suggestion of divine control but we never understand its pattern. On this sea, two human forces, wisdom and chastity, seem to show divine investment, seem to show that the terrible power of the sea can be brought to help the fulfilment of the great triangle of affection represented by Pericles, Thaisa, and Marina.

*

It is only at this point that I think it is right to engage with the question: is *Pericles, Prince of Tyre* by Shakespeare? The play we have described has very close resemblances to *The Winter's Tale*, which Shakespeare wrote in 1610–11, and *The Tempest*, written in 1611–12. In both these plays the sea and voyaging are strongly present, and both are deeply concerned with the relationship of father and daughter.

> *a cherubin*
> *Thou wast that did preserve me . . .*

says Prospero to Miranda, and the arrangement of the marriage of his daughter to Ferdinand is a vital feature of *The Tempest*. The parallels between *Pericles* and *The Winter's Tale* are remarkable. Leontes is separated from his daughter when she is an infant, and she, growing up all innocence and strength among flowers, is restored to him at length. Straight after that restoration, his wife, Hermione, supposed dead, is 'miraculously' revealed to him. There is a union of two couples in two generations, linked by the filial bond. There is a further resemblance, curious and indirect. In *Pandosto*, Shakespeare's source for *The Winter's Tale*, Leontes (to call the characters by the names they have in the play) becomes infatuated with his daughter Perdita, neither knowing who the other is. Though ashamed of such desire at his age, he tries to win her from Florizel by persuasion and threats and make her his concubine. She resists him. When he later learns that the girl he has pursued is his own daughter, 'calling to mind . . . that contrary to the law of nature he had lusted after his own daughter . . . he slew himself.' Shakespeare's play makes a pointed contrast. Though Leontes is moved by Perdita's beauty, and he thinks passingly of her as his queen, the 'heat of unlawful lust' has no place in the affection between father and daughter, each of them with a marriage partner. So, in *The Winter's Tale* as in *Pericles*, the point of departure is an incestuous relationship. Both plays call attention to the long lapse of time in the middle by means of which the girl who was a new-born babe becomes a marriageable young woman in the second half.

The commonest view of Shakespeare's connexion with *Pericles* is that he is responsible for the last three acts, from the storm which sees the birth of Marina and the supposed death of Thaisa (III.1). Certainly from this point there is a big improvement in the language of the Quarto and in the sheer interest of the situations. There are many varieties of this dominant view, and there are other views as well. It has been argued that Shakespeare revised an old play, rewriting the last three acts but only 'touching up' the first two. Some say that the play is a collaboration between Shakespeare and another dramatist (or more than one); or that it is an early play of Shakespeare's which he later rewrote. It has been held that Shakespeare was responsible for the whole play, and also that he wrote none of it. It needs to be said emphatically that all of these theories are tenable, and that not one of them can muster enough evidence to be convincing.

The only real external evidence concerning authorship is the presence of 'By William Shakespeare' on the title-page of the 1609 Quarto, and the absence of the play from the collection of Shakespeare's works in 1623, the 'first Folio'. Neither of these things is proof of authorship or non-authorship. Plays that are definitely not Shakespeare's, like *The London Prodigal* (1605) and *The Yorkshire Tragedy* (1608), carried his name on the title-page, and, although the first Folio contains one play which is a collaboration (*Henry VIII*, with Fletcher), it omits *The Two Noble Kinsmen*, which is also a collaboration between Shakespeare and Fletcher. If it is argued that *Pericles* is wholly by Shakespeare, its omission from the first Folio needs a good deal of explanation because we know of no other play wholly written by Shakespeare which was not included.

Much of the energy and time spent on the subject of Who wrote *Pericles*? has been wasted, because the language of the Quarto has been used as the basis for testing authorship. The Quarto is a debased text and its language is the language of the pirates who got the text together. To what extent that language is likely to be a faithful reproduction of the genuine language is an indispensable preliminary question. Until we are satisfied that we have gone as far as we can in trying to find out how far the original language of the play is likely to have been corrupted or perverted in the course of its transmission, we cannot begin to hand out portions of *Pericles* to various authors on the grounds of style. Anyone who sat down with the bad 1603 text of *Hamlet* before him and tried to find out its author from the evidence of its style would produce ludicrous results.

> *O mother, if ever you did my dear father love,*
> *Forbear the adulterous bed tonight,*
> *And win yourself by little as you may,*
> *In time it may be you will loathe him quite.*
> *And, mother, but assist me in revenge,*
> *And in his death your infamy shall die.*

We still do not know much about how unauthorized play texts came into existence. There is evidence that sometimes shorthand notes were used, that minor actors collaborated, that perhaps clandestine glimpses of playhouse manuscripts, or even bits copied out, went towards the reconstruction of texts. Whatever method was used, memory must have played an important part. It is a hazardous and speculative business analysing the corruption in a text with the aim of assessing how far the original language may have been damaged when there is no alternative text to measure it against. Weaknesses in the language and the action of the Quarto which can be taken as signs of a failure to comprehend or remember what was actually said or done on stage are pointed out in the Account of the Text (pages 195–7) and in the Commentary. Although confusions in the action, sheer nonsense or garbling, repetitions and weak 'fillers' abound through the whole extent of the play, it looks as though a different *kind* of reconstruction is going on in the first two acts from that which is observable in the last three. One hypothetical explanation that can be offered for the difference in the types of weakness in the two halves of the play is that a different method of reconstructing the text was adopted from the beginning of Act III, presumably because a second pirate or reporter joined in or took over the work.

The primary evidence for a change in style in the method of reconstructing is that in the first two acts and the first scene of the third act the verse in the Quarto is, with the exception of a few passages, fairly regular and, by and large, correctly printed. From then on, the verse is metrically irregular and uneven, and most of it is printed as prose or misdivided. The literary quality of the verse in the first two acts, as every reader knows, is vastly inferior to that of the last three acts, although a much greater regularity of metre is observed. Now it can be shown time and again that corruptions in the first two acts are cemented within the metrical structure. But in the last three acts corruptions lie in omissions or additions which destroy the metrical structure. It may be deduced from this important difference that the first two acts of the play represent an unauthorized rewriting in humdrum verse, while the last three acts give an incomplete recording of the original language.

The particularly tell-tale weaknesses in Acts I and II are in rhymed couplets. Here is an example:

> *Opinion's but a fool, that makes us scan*
> *The outward habit by the inward man.*

> II.2.55–6

The idea has been put upside down. 'Opinion' makes us judge the inward man by the outward habit. Wilkins's narrative paraphrases it in this way: 'so the outward habit was the least table of the inward mind.' The reporter working at his text for the Quarto has locked up his error in the rhyme of the couplet; you cannot undo the damage by transposing the words 'inward' and 'outward'. It was not that the reporter damaged an original couplet; rather, the reporter composed a couplet embodying a mistake. Another give-away of the same kind occurs at II.3.43–4:

> *Where now his son's like a glow-worm in the night,*
> *The which hath fire in darkness, none in light.*

This awful couplet embodies in the rhyme-scheme another simple inversion. The eclipsed son is properly a glow-worm *in the day*, temporarily extinguished or invisible.

Beside couplets of this kind one has to put the very many couplets which are clumsy and hobbling in style and almost without meaning.

> *O my distressed lord, even such our griefs are.*
> *Here they are but felt, and seen with mischief's eyes,*
> *But like to groves, being topped, they higher rise.*
>
> I.4.7–9

> *All poverty was scorned, and pride so great,*
> *The name of help grew odious to repeat.* I.4.30–31

> *And with dead cheeks advise thee to desist*
> *For going on death's net, whom none resist.* I.1.40–41

> *we are gentlemen*
> *Have neither in our hearts nor outward eyes*
> *Envie[d] the great nor shall the low despise.* II.3.24–6

Awkwardness and absurdity of this kind give the strong impression that someone has been doing some amateur cobbling and stitching. And indeed so much of the verse in the first two acts is so downright feeble that only the hypothesis of a clumsy rewriting can explain it. A particularly interesting example is in the verse given to Pericles in the fishermen scene (II.1). The prose of the fishermen, though it contains many difficulties which are clear signs of a reported text, is lively and emphatic. But the verse, by contrast, is flat, insipid, commonplace.

> *A man thronged up with cold; my veins are chill,*
> *And have no more of life than may suffice*
> *To give my tongue that heat to ask your help;*
> *Which if you shall refuse, when I am dead,*
> *For that I am a man, pray you see me burièd.*
>
> II.1.73–7

It is hardly conceivable that the man who composed that verse could also create the vivid prose of the fishermen. The prose seems a 'report'; the verse a rewriting. Another sign of rewriting, which we shall come to shortly, is that on many occasions in the first two acts the awkward compression of the verse suggests a frustrated attempt to accommodate someone else's ideas and images. A good example is the following couplet:

> *For death remembered should be like a mirror,*
> *Who tells us life's but breath, to trust it error.*
>
> I.1.46–7

The second line is a weak patching to make up a rhyme. The first line seems to be a compression of the idea that if you look at a skull or 'death's-head' (Pericles is looking at the severed heads of the unsuccessful knights at Antioch), you realize that you are looking at your own image in a mirror. There is better poetry behind the lines of the Quarto than there is in them. Many problems about the first two acts disappear if we accept the hypothesis that some unauthorized person has 'made up' the verse from imperfect notes or a half-remembered original. The deficiencies of the last three acts are of quite another kind, and there seems to be no attempt at writing up, certainly not in couplets. There are descents into commonplace or awkward language which suggest substitutions for or misplacements of a lost original, but the pattern as a whole argues that it is a not unfaithful recollection of original phrases rapidly written down in prose form.

It is an arguable theory, then, that the text of *Pericles* as we have it is an assemblage by two different 'reporters'. The first tried to create a 'literary' wholeness from his notes or memory by refashioning what he had into a rather feeble verse. The second had a livelier understanding and better notes or recollection and has given us material which, while it is extremely irregular as verse, preserves more of the original wording than the rewriting of Acts I and II does. Only in the first scene of Act III, where the verse is fairly regular, does one have the feeling that we may be very near the original text. Many would say that it is the best scene in the play; it would be more cautious to say that it is the best-reported.

If the major responsibility for the feebleness of language in the first two acts belongs to the reporter, we must be very careful indeed before we assert that the difference in style between Acts I–II and Acts III–V is the result of collaboration, and that it is at Act III, scene 1, that Shakespeare takes over. Every reader feels the relief and pleasure of emerging from the dogged jog-trot of the verse of the early part to the beauty of the 'sea-music' of the tragic storm, with Pericles' vision of Thaisa's corpse 'Lying with simple shells'. If this is not Shakespeare, it is surely near-Shakespeare. But our pleasure may be not that of greeting a better dramatist, but that of getting rid of the ineptitude of the first pirate.

I do not think it can be maintained that the whole of the original *Pericles* as acted was by Shakespeare. But it must always be borne in mind that there is a wholeness in the design of the play, a consistency in its method and a unity in its meaning, which powerfully suggests that the play was conceived as a whole by a single mind. And the comparison with *The Winter's Tale* and *The Tempest* leaves me in no doubt whatsoever that that mind was Shakespeare's. A second proposition which may be borne in mind is this. It has been argued that the verse of Acts I and II is a reworking of verse which was once much better. Now, while such archaeological work is very tricky and uncertain, a reader must often have the feeling that what lay behind the different individual scenes of the first two acts was not all of the same quality. And he may feel that there are some scenes in the later acts which, while much higher in quality than the general run of Acts I and II, are still without much evidence of being by Shakespeare.

About five years after *Pericles* was performed, Shakespeare engaged in a collaboration with John Fletcher to write *The Two Noble Kinsmen*, which was also based on a famous and ancient story retold by a medieval poet (Chaucer). Its design seems quite certainly Shakespeare's. In many of the intermediary scenes one feels that Fletcher's fluent and theatrical writing has diluted the grand design. In this play, as in Shakespeare's other collaboration with Fletcher, *Henry VIII*, the master introduced the work by writing the first scene. The situation with *Pericles* may have been much as it was with *The Two Noble Kinsmen*. It is in the first scene that one most often feels that powerful imagery and language have been blunted, cheapened, telescoped, and confused. It is in this scene that we get the image of death and the mirror already noticed, and the famous passage about the blind mole:

> The blind mole casts
> Copped hills towards heaven, to tell the earth is thronged
> By man's oppression, and the poor worm doth die for't.
>
> I.I.101–3

Just before this, there is a curiously muddled section about vice and the wind. It looks as though in Pericles' speeches whole sequences of vivid images have left the reporter quite at sea in a kind of language altogether beyond his grasp, or certainly his power to reproduce. One does not have the same feeling of ruined greatness in other scenes of Act I. They are often very corrupt, but there are few buried nuggets like the 'blind mole' passage. In the second act, the scene with the fishermen is not only good in itself, but carries suggestions that the original was even better, especially in the sardonic character of the Second Fisherman. It may be, then, that *Pericles*, like *The Two Noble Kinsmen* and *Henry VIII*, was the work of Shakespeare and a collaborator; that Shakespeare wrote the first scene of the first act and the first scene of the second act (the fishermen scene); that he wrote most of the last three acts, but that the collaborator was present here too, writing perhaps the scene between Cleon and Dionyza (IV.3).

The Gower choruses are a special problem. There are seven of them. It is often said that the chorus which opens Act III is obviously *better* than those of the first two acts. But these choruses are corrupt and suffer from as much unhappy rewriting as the text itself, and the studied naivety and rough archaizing of all the choruses which open the first four acts are not really dissimilar in what we can perceive of their intended language, tone, and form. The last three choruses (IV.4, V Chorus, and the Epilogue) are very different. They abandon the octosyllabic couplet (which is the metre of Gower's own version in *Confessio Amantis*) and introduce the decasyllabic line, twice employing couplets and once using the quatrain form, *abab*. No attempt is made to maintain an archaic diction. These last three choruses may well be the work of the collaborator.

It is impossible to name this putative collaborator. Thomas Heywood, John Day, Samuel Rowley, George Wilkins have all been proposed as part-authors of *Pericles*. But since these proposals have been made on the ground of linguistic similarities, they all suffer from the drawback that one arm of the comparison is not the original style at all but a clumsy repair. One has to admit, regretfully, that the problem is insoluble because the authentic text is irrecoverable. But that Shakespeare had a large share in the conception of the play and in the writing of it seems indisputable. The objection to the view that he revised an earlier play by another dramatist and confined his re-writing largely to the last three acts is that the archaic naivety which he is thus supposed to have started to brush up is part and parcel of the very meaning of the play. It would be curious indeed if Shakespeare had discovered, in a poor play that he started tinkering with, the kind of plot, the kind of art, the kind of theme, which he was to spend all the endeavour of the last years of his writing life trying to develop. It would be curious, but it has to be admitted it would not be impossible. There is no solution to the problems of *Pericles*.

FURTHER READING

Texts

A photographic facsimile of the 1609 Quarto with an introduction by W. W. Greg (1940) is in the Oxford series of
Shakespeare Quarto Facsimiles. J. C. Maxwell's edition of the
play in the New Cambridge Shakespeare (1956) is outstanding
for its discernment and good judgement. It has been followed
by F. D. Hoeniger's edition in the new Arden Shakespeare
(London, 1963), which has a full and informative introduction,
and Ernest Schanzer's in the Signet Shakespeare (New York,
1965), which packs much fresh thought into small compass.

The introductions to the last three editions carry further the
debate about the quality and provenance of the text initiated in
Philip Edwards's 'An Approach to the Problem of *Pericles*', in
Shakespeare Survey 5 (Cambridge, 1952).

Sources and Analogues

An admirable and comprehensive study of the sources is available in Volume VI (London, 1966) of Geoffrey Bullough's
Narrative and Dramatic Sources of Shakespeare. Bullough
prints the texts of Gower and Twine, and also gives the
indispensable analogue, George Wilkins's *The Painful Adventures of Pericles, Prince of Tyre*. The latter has also been edited
with an introduction by Kenneth Muir (Liverpool, 1953). The
history of the tale of Apollonius of Tyre is studied in Albert H.
Smyth's *Shakespeare's 'Pericles' and Apollonius of Tyre*
(Philadelphia, 1898).

Criticism

G. Wilson Knight as pioneer must head any list of modern
criticism of *Pericles*. His thoughts on the symbolic power of
the play from the late 1920s onwards can be seen in *The Crown*

of Life (London, 1947). J. F. Danby's *Poets on Fortune's Hill* (London, 1952; reprinted as *Elizabethan and Jacobean Poets*) contains a useful study of how the moral functions of romance are deployed in *Pericles*; an extract is reprinted in *Shakespeare's Later Comedies: An Anthology of Modern Criticism*, edited by D. J. Palmer (Penguin Shakespeare Library, Harmondsworth, 1971). D. A. Traversi's discussion of the moral pattern and the poetic symbolism of the play in *Shakespeare: The Last Phase* (London, 1954) puts a different view of Marina's trials in the brothel from that advanced in the Introduction to this edition, criticizing them as 'excessively facile and sentimental'.

John Arthos's '*Pericles, Prince of Tyre*: A Study in the Dramatic Use of Romantic Narrative', in *Shakespeare Quarterly* 4 (1953), is an excellent essay to which the present editor is deeply indebted. Another very good study of the play, with an examination of the authorship problem, is in Kenneth Muir's *Shakespeare as Collaborator* (London, 1960). Northrop Frye has a good deal to say about *Pericles* in his book on comedy and romance in Shakespeare, *A Natural Perspective* (New York, 1965), and he is both original and provocative. An interesting view of what Shakespeare intended by his use of the incest-motif is C. L. Barber's essay ' "Thou that beget'st him that did thee beget"; Transformation in *Pericles* and *The Winter's Tale*', *Shakespeare Survey 22* (Cambridge, 1969).

PERICLES, PRINCE OF TYRE

THE CHARACTERS IN THE PLAY

John GOWER, the presenter

ANTIOCHUS, King of Antioch
PERICLES, Prince of Tyre
DAUGHTER of Antiochus
THALIARD, a lord of Antioch
MESSENGER of Antioch

HELICANUS
ESCANES } lords of Tyre
Other LORDS of Tyre

CLEON, governor of Tarsus
DIONYZA, wife of Cleon
LORD of Tarsus

Three FISHERMEN of Pentapolis
SIMONIDES, King of Pentapolis
THAISA, daughter of Simonides
Three LORDS of Pentapolis
Five KNIGHTS
MARSHAL

LYCHORIDA, a nurse
Two SAILORS

CERIMON, a lord of Ephesus
Two SERVANTS of Ephesus

THE CHARACTERS IN THE PLAY

PHILEMON, servant of Cerimon
Two GENTLEMEN of Ephesus

LEONINE, servant of Dionyza
MARINA, daughter of Pericles
Three PIRATES

PANDER
BAWD
BOULT, servant of the Pander and the Bawd
Two GENTLEMEN of Mytilene
LYSIMACHUS, governor of Mytilene

SAILOR of Tyre
SAILOR of Mytilene
GENTLEMAN of Tyre
LORD of Mytilene

DIANA, goddess of chastity

Messengers, gentlemen, lords, ladies, attendants, servants, companion of Marina, priestesses, inhabitants of Ephesus

I chorus

Enter Gower

GOWER

To sing a song that old was sung,
From ashes ancient Gower is come,
Assuming man's infirmities,
To glad your ear and please your eyes.
It hath been sung at festivals,
On ember-eves and holidays,
And lords and ladies in their lives
Have read it for restoratives.
The purchase is to make men glorious,
Et bonum quo antiquius eo melius.   10
If you, born in these latter times
When wit's more ripe, accept my rhymes,
And that to hear an old man sing
May to your wishes pleasure bring,
I life would wish, and that I might
Waste it for you like taper-light.
This Antioch, then. Antiochus the Great
Built up this city for his chiefest seat,
The fairest in all Syria;
I tell you what mine authors say.   20
This king unto him took a peer,
Who died and left a female heir,
So buxom, blithe, and full of face
As heaven had lent her all his grace;
With whom the father liking took,
And her to incest did provoke.

49

morality

Bad child, worse father, to entice his own
To evil should be done by none;
But custom what they did begin
30   Was with long use accounted no sin.
The beauty of this sinful dame
Made many princes thither frame
To seek her as a bedfellow,
In marriage pleasures playfellow;
Which to prevent he made a law,
To keep her still and men in awe,
That whoso asked her for his wife,
His riddle told not, lost his life.
So for her many a wight did die,
40   As yon grim looks do testify.
What now ensues, to the judgement of your eye –
I give my cause, who best can justify.   *Exit*

I.1   *Enter Antiochus, Prince Pericles, and followers*

ANTIOCHUS
Young Prince of Tyre, you have at large received
The danger of the task you undertake?

PERICLES
I have, Antiochus, and with a soul
Emboldened with the glory of her praise
Think death no hazard in this enterprise.

ANTIOCHUS
Music!
Bring in our daughter, clothèd like a bride
For embracements even of Jove himself,
At whose conception, till Lucina reigned,
10   Nature this dowry gave; to glad her presence,
The senate-house of planets all did sit
To knit in her their best perfections.

Enter Antiochus's Daughter

PERICLES

See where she comes, apparelled like the spring,
Graces her subjects, and her thoughts the king
Of every virtue gives renown to men;
Her face the book of praises, where is read
Nothing but curious pleasures, as from thence
Sorrow were ever razed, and testy wrath
Could never be her mild companion.
You gods that made me man, and sway in love,   20
That have inflamed desire in my breast
To taste the fruit of yon celestial tree
Or die in the adventure, be my helps,
As I am son and servant to your will,
To compass such a boundless happiness!

ANTIOCHUS

Prince Pericles –

PERICLES

That would be son to great Antiochus.

ANTIOCHUS

Before thee stands this fair Hesperides,
With golden fruit, but dangerous to be touched,
For deathlike dragons here affright thee hard.   30
Her face, like heaven, enticeth thee to view
Her countless glory, which desert must gain;
And which without desert because thine eye
Presumes to reach, all the whole heap must die.
Yon sometimes famous princes, like thyself,
Drawn by report, adventurous by desire,
Tell thee with speechless tongues and semblance pale
That without covering, save yon field of stars,
Here they stand martyrs slain in Cupid's wars;
And with dead cheeks advise thee to desist   40
For going on death's net, whom none resist.

PERICLES

    Antiochus, I thank thee, who hath taught
    My frail mortality to know itself,
    And by those fearful objects to prepare
    This body, like to them, to what I must;
    For death remembered should be like a mirror,
    Who tells us life's but breath, to trust it error.
    I'll make my will then, and as sick men do,
    Who know the world, see heaven, but feeling woe
50   Gripe not at earthly joys as erst they did,
    So I bequeath a happy peace to you
    And all good men, as every prince should do;
    My riches to the earth from whence they came,
    (*to the Daughter*)
    But my unspotted fire of love to you.
    Thus ready for the way of life or death,
    I wait the sharpest blow, Antiochus.

ANTIOCHUS

    Scorning advice, read the conclusion then,
    Which read and not expounded, 'tis decreed,
    As these before thee, thou thyself shalt bleed.

DAUGHTER

60   Of all 'sayed yet, mayst thou prove prosperous!
    Of all 'sayed yet, I wish thee happiness.

PERICLES

    Like a bold champion I assume the lists,
    Nor ask advice of any other thought
    But faithfulness and courage.
       He reads aloud

THE RIDDLE

I am no viper, yet I feed
On mother's flesh which did me breed.
I sought a husband, in which labour
I found that kindness in a father.

> *He's father, son, and husband mild;*
> *I mother, wife, and yet his child.*   70
> *How they may be, and yet in two,*
> *As you will live, resolve it you.*

(*Aside*) Sharp physic is the last. But O you powers
That gives heaven countless eyes to view men's acts,
Why cloud they not their sights perpetually,
If this be true which makes me pale to read it?
Fair glass of light, I loved you, and could still,
Were not this glorious casket stored with ill.
But I must tell you now my thoughts revolt;
For he's no man on whom perfections wait   80
That, knowing sin within, will touch the gate.
You are a fair viol, and your sense the strings,
Who, fingered to make man his lawful music,
Would draw heaven down and all the gods to hearken,
But, being played upon before your time,
Hell only danceth at so harsh a chime.
Good sooth, I care not for you.

ANTIOCHUS

Prince Pericles, touch not, upon thy life,
For that's an article within our law
As dangerous as the rest. Your time's expired;   90
Either expound now or receive your sentence.

PERICLES

Great King,
Few love to hear the sins they love to act.
'Twould braid yourself too near for me to tell it.
Who has a book of all that monarchs do,
He's more secure to keep it shut than shown,
For vice repeated is like the wandering wind,
Blows dust in others' eyes to spread itself;
And yet the end of all is bought thus dear,

100   The breath is gone, and the sore eyes see clear
      To stop the air would hurt them. The blind mole casts
      Copped hills towards heaven, to tell the earth is thronged
      By man's oppression, and the poor worm doth die for't.
      Kings are earth's gods; in vice, their law's their will;
      And if Jove stray, who dares say Jove doth ill?
      It is enough you know, and it is fit,
      What being more known grows worse, to smother it.
      All love the womb that their first being bred;
      Then give my tongue like leave to love my head.

ANTIOCHUS (*aside*)

110   Heaven, that I had thy head! He has found the meaning.
      But I will gloze with him. – Young Prince of Tyre,
      Though by the tenor of our strict edict,
      Your exposition misinterpreting,
      We might proceed to cancel of your days,
      Yet hope, succeeding from so fair a tree
      As your fair self, doth tune us otherwise.
      Forty days longer we do respite you,
      If by which time our secret be undone,
      This mercy shows we'll joy in such a son.

120   And until then your entertain shall be
      As doth befit our honour and your worth.

                       Exeunt. Pericles remains alone

PERICLES

      How courtesy would seem to cover sin,
      When what is done is like an hypocrite,
      The which is good in nothing but in sight.
      If it be true that I interpret false,
      Then were it certain you were not so bad
      As with foul incest to abuse your soul;
      Where now you're both a father and a son
      By your untimely claspings with your child,

130   Which pleasures fits a husband, not a father;

And she an eater of her mother's flesh
By the defiling of her parents' bed;
And both like serpents are, who, though they feed
On sweetest flowers, yet they poison breed.
Antioch, farewell, for wisdom sees those men
Blush not in actions blacker than the night
Will shun no course to keep them from the light.
One sin, I know, another doth provoke.
Murder's as near to lust as flame to smoke.
Poison and treason are the hands of sin,   140
Ay, and the targets to put off the shame.
Then, lest my life be cropped to keep you clear,
By flight I'll shun the danger which I fear.   *Exit*
    Enter Antiochus

ANTIOCHUS
He hath found the meaning,
For which we mean to have his head.
He must not live to trumpet forth my infamy,
Nor tell the world Antiochus doth sin
In such a loathèd manner.
And therefore instantly this prince must die,
For by his fall my honour must keep high.   150
Who attends us there?
    Enter Thaliard

THALIARD   Doth your highness call?
ANTIOCHUS
Thaliard, you are of our chamber, Thaliard,
And our mind partakes her private actions
To your secrecy; and for your faithfulness
We will advance you, Thaliard.
Behold, here's poison, and here's gold.
We hate the Prince of Tyre, and thou must kill him.
It fits thee not to ask the reason why,
Because we bid it. Say, is it done?

THALIARD
  My lord, 'tis done.

160 ANTIOCHUS   Enough.
          Enter a Messenger
  Let your breath cool yourself, telling your haste.

MESSENGER My lord, Prince Pericles is fled.   *Exit*

ANTIOCHUS As thou wilt live, fly after, and like an arrow
  shot from a well-experienced archer hits the mark his
  eye doth level at, so thou never return unless thou say
  'Prince Pericles is dead.'

THALIARD My lord, if I can get him within my pistol's
  length, I'll make him sure enough. So farewell to your
  highness.

ANTIOCHUS
  Thaliard, adieu.   *Exit Thaliard*

170   Till Pericles be dead,
  My heart can lend no succour to my head.   *Exit*

I.2   *Enter Pericles with his Lords*

PERICLES
  Let none disturb us.   *Exeunt Lords*
              Why should this change of thoughts,
  The sad companion, dull-eyed melancholy,
  Be my so used a guest as not an hour
  In the day's glorious walk or peaceful night,
  The tomb where grief should sleep, can breed me
          quiet?
  Here pleasures court mine eyes, and mine eyes shun
          them,
  And danger, which I feared, is at Antioch,
  Whose arm seems far too short to hit me here.
  Yet neither pleasure's art can joy my spirits,
10 Nor yet the other's distance comfort me.

Then it is thus: the passions of the mind,
That have their first conception by misdread,
Have after-nourishment and life by care,
And what was first but fear what might be done
Grows elder now and cares it be not done;
And so with me. The great Antiochus,
'Gainst whom I am too little to contend,
Since he's so great can make his will his act,
Will think me speaking, though I swear to silence;
Nor boots it me to say I honour   20
If he suspect I may dishonour him.
And what may make him blush in being known,
He'll stop the course by which it might be known.
With hostile forces he'll o'erspread the land,
And with the ostent of war will look so huge
Amazement shall drive courage from the state,
Our men be vanquished ere they do resist,
And subjects punished that ne'er thought offence;
Which care of them, not pity of myself,
Who am no more but as the tops of trees   30
Which fence the roots they grow by and defend them,
Makes both my body pine and soul to languish,
And punish that before that he would punish.
        Enter Helicanus and the Lords

FIRST LORD
Joy and all comfort in your sacred breast!
SECOND LORD
And keep your mind till you return to us
Peaceful and comfortable.
HELICANUS
Peace, peace, and give experience tongue.
They do abuse the king that flatter him,
For flattery is the bellows blows up sin;
The thing the which is flattered, but a spark,   40

57

To which that wind gives heat and stronger glowing;
Whereas reproof, obedient and in order,
Fits kings as they are men, for they may err.
When Signor Sooth here does proclaim peace,
He flatters you, makes war upon your life.
Prince, pardon me, or strike me if you please;
I cannot be much lower than my knees.

He kneels

PERICLES

All leave us else. But let your cares o'erlook
What shipping and what lading's in our haven,
And then return to us.   *Exeunt Lords*

50   Helicanus,
Thou hast moved us. What seest thou in our looks?

HELICANUS

An angry brow, dread lord.

PERICLES

If there be such a dart in princes' frowns,
How durst thy tongue move anger to our face?

HELICANUS

How dares the plants look up to heaven,
From whence they have their nourishment?

PERICLES

Thou knowest I have power to take thy life from thee.

HELICANUS

I have ground the axe myself. Do but you strike the
blow.

PERICLES

Rise, prithee rise. Sit down. Thou art no flatterer;
60   I thank thee for't, and heaven forbid
That kings should let their ears hear their faults hid.
Fit counsellor and servant for a prince,
Who by thy wisdom makes a prince thy servant,
What wouldst thou have me do?

HELICANUS

To bear with patience such griefs
As you yourself do lay upon yourself.

PERICLES

Thou speakest like a physician, Helicanus,
That ministers a potion unto me
That thou wouldst tremble to receive thyself.
Attend me then. I went to Antioch,   70
Where, as thou knowest, against the face of death
I sought the purchase of a glorious beauty,
From whence an issue I might propagate,
Are arms to princes and bring joys to subjects.
Her face was to mine eye beyond all wonder, ·
The rest – hark in thine ear – as black as incest;
Which by my knowledge found, the sinful father
Seemed not to strike, but smooth. But thou knowest
        this,
'Tis time to fear when tyrants seems to kiss.
Which fear so grew in me I hither fled   80
Under the covering of a careful night
Who seemed my good protector; and, being here,
Bethought me what was past, what might succeed.
I knew him tyrannous, and tyrants' fears
Decrease not, but grow faster than the years.
And should he doubt, as no doubt he doth,
That I should open to the listening air
How many worthy princes' bloods were shed
To keep his bed of blackness unlaid ope,
To lop that doubt, he'll fill this land with arms,   90
And make pretence of wrong that I have done him,
When all for mine – if I may call – offence
Must feel war's blow, who spares not innocence;
Which love to all, of which thyself art one,
Who now reprovedst me for't –

HELICANUS   Alas, sir!
PERICLES
    Drew sleep out of mine eyes, blood from my cheeks,
    Musings into my mind, with thousand doubts,
    How I might stop this tempest ere it came;
    And, finding little comfort to relieve them,
100   I thought it princely charity to grieve for them.
HELICANUS
    Well, my lord, since you have given me leave to speak,
    Freely will I speak. Antiochus you fear,
    And justly too, I think, you fear the tyrant
    Who either by public war or private treason
    Will take away your life.
    Therefore, my lord, go travel for a while,
    Till that his rage and anger be forgot,
    Or till the destinies do cut his thread of life.
    Your rule direct to any; if to me,
110   Day serves not light more faithful than I'll be.
PERICLES
    I do not doubt thy faith,
    But should he wrong my liberties in my absence?
HELICANUS
    We'll mingle our bloods together in the earth,
    From whence we had our being and our birth.
PERICLES
    Tyre, I now look from thee then, and to Tarsus
    Intend my travel, where I'll hear from thee,
    And by whose letters I'll dispose myself.
    The care I had and have of subjects' good
    On thee I lay, whose wisdom's strength can bear it.
120   I'll take thy word for faith, not ask thine oath;
    Who shuns not to break one will crack both.
    But in our orbs we'll live so round and safe
    That time of both this truth shall ne'er convince,

Thou showedst a subject's shine, I a true prince.

Exeunt

Enter Thaliard alone   I.3

THALIARD So this is Tyre, and this the court. Here must
I kill King Pericles; and if I do it not, I am sure to be
hanged at home. 'Tis dangerous. Well, I perceive he
was a wise fellow and had good discretion that, being
bid to ask what he would of the king, desired he might
know none of his secrets. Now do I see he had some
reason for't, for if a king bid a man be a villain, he's
bound by the indenture of his oath to be one. Husht!
Here comes the lords of Tyre.

Enter Helicanus and Escanes, with other lords

HELICANUS

You shall not need, my fellow peers of Tyre,   10
Further to question me of your King's departure.
His sealed commission, left in trust with me,
Does speak sufficiently he's gone to travel.

THALIARD (*aside*) How? the King gone?

HELICANUS

If further yet you will be satisfied
Why, as it were, unlicensed of your loves
He would depart, I'll give some light unto you.
Being at Antioch –

THALIARD (*aside*)   What from Antioch?

HELICANUS

Royal Antiochus, on what cause I know not,
Took some displeasure at him; at least he judged so.   20
And doubting lest he had erred or sinned,
To show his sorrow he'd correct himself;
So puts himself unto the shipman's toil,
With whom each minute threatens life or death.

THALIARD (*aside*) Well, I perceive I shall not be hanged
now although I would; but since he's gone, the King's
seas must please; he 'scaped the land to perish at the
sea. I'll present myself.

He comes forward

Peace to the lords of Tyre!

HELICANUS

30   Lord Thaliard from Antiochus is welcome.

THALIARD

From him I come
With message unto princely Pericles,
But since my landing I have understood
Your lord has betaken himself to unknown travels.
Now my message must return from whence it came.

HELICANUS

We have no reason to desire it,
Commended to our master, not to us.
Yet, ere you shall depart, this we desire,
As friends to Antioch, we may feast in Tyre.   *Exeunt*

I.4   *Enter Cleon, the Governor of Tarsus, with Dionyza,*
his wife, and others

CLEON

My Dionyza, shall we rest us here
And, by relating tales of others' griefs,
See if 'twill teach us to forget our own?

DIONYZA

Fire   That were to blow at fire in hope to quench it,
For who digs hills because they do aspire
Throws down one mountain to cast up a higher.
O my distressed lord, even such our griefs are.
Here they are but felt, and seen with mischief's eyes,
But like to groves, being topped, they higher rise.

CLEON

    O Dionyza,   10

    Who wanteth food and will not say he wants it,

    Or can conceal his hunger till he famish?

    Our tongues and sorrows force us to sound deep

    Our woes into the air, our eyes to weep,

    Till tongues fetch breath that may proclaim them
           louder,

    That, if heaven slumber while their creatures want,

    They may awake their helpers to comfort them.

    I'll then discourse our woes, felt several years,

    And, wanting breath to speak, help me with tears.

DIONYZA

    I'll do my best, sir.   20

CLEON

    This Tarsus, o'er which I have the government,

    A city on whom plenty held full hand,

    For riches strewed herself even in her streets,

    Whose towers bore heads so high they kissed the clouds,

    And strangers ne'er beheld but wondered at,

    Whose men and dames so jetted and adorned,

    Like one another's glass to trim them by;

    Their tables were stored full, to glad the sight,

    And not so much to feed on as delight;

    All poverty was scorned, and pride so great,   30

    The name of help grew odious to repeat.

DIONYZA

    O, 'tis too true!

CLEON

    But see what heaven can do by this our change.

    These mouths who but of late earth, sea, and air

    Were all too little to content and please,

    Although they gave their creatures in abundance,

    As houses are defiled for want of use,

They are now starved for want of exercise.
Those palates who, not yet two summers younger,
40 Must have inventions to delight the taste
Would now be glad of bread and beg for it.
Those mothers who to nuzzle up their babes
Thought naught too curious are ready now
To eat those little darlings whom they loved.
So sharp are hunger's teeth that man and wife
Draw lots who first shall die to lengthen life.
Here stands a lord and there a lady weeping;
Here many sink, yet those which see them fall
Have scarce strength left to give them burial.
50 Is not this true?

DIONYZA
Our cheeks and hollow eyes do witness it.

CLEON
O, let those cities that of plenty's cup
And her prosperities so largely taste
With their superfluous riots, hear these tears!
The misery of Tarsus may be theirs.

Enter a Lord

LORD
Where's the lord governor?

CLEON
Here.
Speak out thy sorrows which thou bringest in haste,
For comfort is too far for us to expect.

LORD
60 We have descried, upon our neighbouring shore,
A portly sail of ships make hitherward.

CLEON
I thought as much.
One sorrow never comes but brings an heir
That may succeed as his inheritor,

And so in ours. Some neighbouring nation,
Taking advantage of our misery,
Hath stuffed the hollow vessels with their power,
To beat us down, the which are down already,
And make a conquest of unhappy me,
Whereas no glory's got to overcome.   70

LORD

That's the least fear, for by the semblance
Of their white flags displayed they bring us peace,
And come to us as favourers, not as foes.

CLEON

Thou speakest like him's untutored to repeat:
Who makes the fairest show means most deceit.
But bring they what they will and what they can,
What need we fear?
Our ground's the lowest and we are half-way there.
Go tell their general we attend him here,
To know for what he comes and whence he comes   80
And what he craves.

LORD

I go, my lord.   *Exit*

CLEON

Welcome is peace if he on peace consist;
If wars, we are unable to resist.
     Enter Pericles with attendants

PERICLES

Lord governor, for so we hear you are,
Let not our ships and number of our men
Be like a beacon fired t'amaze your eyes.
We have heard your miseries as far as Tyre
And seen the desolation of your streets;
Nor come we to add sorrow to your tears,   90
But to relieve them of their heavy load;
And these our ships you happily may think

Are like the Trojan horse, was stuffed within
With bloody veins expecting overthrow,
Are stored with corn to make your needy bread
And give them life whom hunger starved half dead.

ALL

The gods of Greece protect you!
And we'll pray for you.

They kneel

PERICLES   Arise, I pray you, rise.

We do not look for reverence but for love,

100   And harbourage for ourself, our ships, and men.

CLEON

The which when any shall not gratify,
Or pay you with unthankfulness in thought,
Be it our wives, our children, or ourselves,
The curse of heaven and men succeed their evils!
Till when – the which I hope shall ne'er be seen –
Your grace is welcome to our town and us.

PERICLES

Which welcome we'll accept, feast here awhile,
Until our stars that frown lend us a smile.   *Exeunt*

*

II CHORUS

Enter Gower

GOWER

Here have you seen a mighty king
His child, iwis, to incest bring;
A better prince and benign lord
That will prove awful both in deed and word.
Be quiet then as men should be

66

Till he hath passed necessity.
I'll show you those in trouble's reign,
Losing a mite, a mountain gain.
The good in conversation,
To whom I give my benison,   10
Is still at Tarsus, where each man
Thinks all is writ he speken can,
And to remember what he does
Build his statue to make him glorious.
But tidings to the contrary
Are brought your eyes; what need speak I?

> *Dumb show:*
> *Enter at one door Pericles talking with Cleon, all the*
> *train with them. Enter at another door a gentleman*
> *with a letter to Pericles. Pericles shows the letter to*
> *Cleon. Pericles gives the messenger a reward and*
> *knights him. Exit Pericles at one door and Cleon at*
> *another*

Good Helicane that stayed at home,
Not to eat honey like a drone
From others' labours, forthy he strive
To killen bad, keep good alive,   20
And to fulfil his prince' desire
Sends word of all that haps in Tyre;
How Thaliard came full bent with sin
And hid intent to murder him,
And that in Tarsus was not best
Longer for him to make his rest.
He, doing so, put forth to seas,
Where, when men been, there's seldom ease;
For now the wind begins to blow;
Thunder above and deeps below   30
Makes such unquiet that the ship
Should house him safe is wracked and split,

67

And he, good prince, having all lost,
By waves from coast to coast is tossed.
All perishen of man, of pelf,
Ne aught escapend but himself;
Till Fortune, tired with doing bad,
Threw him ashore, to give him glad.
And here he comes. What shall be next,
40   Pardon old Gower – this longs the text.   *Exit*

II.1   *Enter Pericles, wet*

PERICLES
   Yet cease your ire, you angry stars of heaven!
   Wind, rain, and thunder, remember earthly man
   Is but a substance that must yield to you,
   And I, as fits my nature, do obey you.
   Alas, the seas hath cast me on the rocks,
   Washed me from shore to shore, and left my breath
   Nothing to think on but ensuing death.
   Let it suffice the greatness of your powers
   To have bereft a prince of all his fortunes,
10   And having thrown him from your watery grave
   Here to have death in peace is all he'll crave.
            He lies down
            Enter three Fishermen

FIRST FISHERMAN What ho, Pilch!

SECOND FISHERMAN Ha, come and bring away the nets!

FIRST FISHERMAN What, Patchbreech, I say!

THIRD FISHERMAN What say you, master?

FIRST FISHERMAN Look how thou stirrest now! Come
   away, or I'll fetch thee with a wanion.

THIRD FISHERMAN Faith, master, I am thinking of the
   poor men that were cast away before us even now.

20 FIRST FISHERMAN Alas, poor souls, it grieved my heart

68

to hear what pitiful cries they made to us to help them,
when, well-a-day, we could scarce help ourselves.

THIRD FISHERMAN Nay, master, said not I as much
when I saw the porpoise how he bounced and tumbled?
They say they're half fish, half flesh. A plague on them,
they ne'er come but I look to be washed. Master, I
marvel how the fishes live in the sea?

FIRST FISHERMAN Why, as men do a-land: the great
ones eat up the little ones. I can compare our rich
misers to nothing so fitly as to a whale: 'a plays and 30
tumbles, driving the poor fry before him, and at last
devour them all at a mouthful. Such whales have I heard
on a-th'land who never leave gaping till they swallowed
the whole parish, church, steeple, bells, and all.

PERICLES (*aside*) A pretty moral!

THIRD FISHERMAN But, master, if I had been the
sexton, I would have been that day in the belfry.

SECOND FISHERMAN Why, man?

THIRD FISHERMAN Because he should have swallowed
me too, and when I had been in his belly I would have 40
kept such a jangling of the bells that he should never
have left till he cast bells, steeple, church, and parish up
again. But if the good King Simonides were of my
mind –

PERICLES (*aside*) Simonides?

THIRD FISHERMAN We would purge the land of these
drones that rob the bee of her honey.

PERICLES (*aside*)
How from the finny subject of the sea
These fishers tell the infirmities of men,
And from their watery empire recollect
All that may men approve or men detect! – 50
Peace be at your labour, honest fishermen!

SECOND FISHERMAN Honest, good fellow? What's

that? If it be a day fits you, search out of the calendar,
and nobody look after it.

PERICLES

May see the sea hath cast upon your coast –

SECOND FISHERMAN What a drunken knave was the sea
to cast thee in our way!

PERICLES

A man whom both the waters and the wind,
60 In that vast tennis-court, hath made the ball
For them to play upon entreats you pity him.
He asks of you that never used to beg.

FIRST FISHERMAN No, friend, cannot you beg? Here's
them in our country of Greece gets more with begging
than we can do with working.

SECOND FISHERMAN Canst thou catch any fishes then?

PERICLES I never practised it.

SECOND FISHERMAN Nay then, thou wilt starve, sure,
for here's nothing to be got nowadays unless thou canst
70 fish for't.

PERICLES

What I have been I have forgot to know;
But what I am, want teaches me to think on:
A man thronged up with cold; my veins are chill,
And have no more of life than may suffice
To give my tongue that heat to ask your help;
Which if you shall refuse, when I am dead,
For that I am a man, pray you see me burièd.

FIRST FISHERMAN Die, quotha! Now gods forbid it an I
have a gown here! Come, put it on, keep thee warm.
80 Now, afore me, a handsome fellow! Come, thou shalt go
home, and we'll have flesh for holidays, fish for fasting-
days, and moreo'er puddings and flapjacks, and thou
shalt be welcome.

PERICLES I thank you, sir.

SECOND FISHERMAN Hark you, my friend, you said you could not beg?

PERICLES I did but crave.

SECOND FISHERMAN But crave? Then I'll turn craver too, and so I shall 'scape whipping.

PERICLES Why, are your beggars whipped then?   90

SECOND FISHERMAN O, not all, my friend, not all, for if all your beggars were whipped, I would wish no better office than to be beadle. But, master, I'll go draw up the net.   *Exeunt Second and Third Fishermen*

PERICLES (*aside*)
How well this honest mirth becomes their labour!

FIRST FISHERMAN Hark you, sir, do you know where ye are?

PERICLES Not well.

FIRST FISHERMAN Why, I'll tell you. This is called Pentapolis, and our king the good Simonides.   100

PERICLES The good Simonides do you call him?

FIRST FISHERMAN Ay, sir, and he deserves so to be called for his peaceable reign and good government.

PERICLES He is a happy king, since he gains from his subjects the name of good by his government. How far is his court distant from this shore?

FIRST FISHERMAN Marry, sir, half a day's journey. And I'll tell you, he hath a fair daughter, and tomorrow is her birthday, and there are princes and knights come from all parts of the world to joust and tourney for her   110 love.

PERICLES Were my fortunes equal to my desires, I could wish to make one there.

FIRST FISHERMAN O, sir, things must be as they may; and what a man cannot get, he may lawfully deal for his wife's soul.

Enter the two Fishermen, drawing up a net

SECOND FISHERMAN Help, master, help! Here's a fish

hangs in the net like a poor man's right in the law; 'twill
hardly come out. Ha, bots on't, 'tis come at last, and 'tis
120 turned to a rusty armour.

PERICLES

An armour, friends? I pray you let me see it.
Thanks, Fortune, yet that after all thy crosses
Thou givest me somewhat to repair myself,
And though it was mine own, part of my heritage,
Which my dead father did bequeath to me,
With this strict charge, even as he left his life:
'Keep it, my Pericles; it hath been a shield
'Twixt me and death', and pointed to this brace,
'For that it saved me, keep it. In like necessity,
130 The which the gods protect thee from, may't defend thee.'
It kept where I kept, I so dearly loved it,
Till the rough seas, that spares not any man,
Took it in rage, though calmed have given't again.
I thank thee for't. My shipwreck now's no ill,
Since I have here my father gave in his will.

FIRST FISHERMAN What mean you, sir?

PERICLES

To beg of you, kind friends, this coat of worth,
For it was sometime target to a king.
I know it by this mark. He loved me dearly,
140 And for his sake I wish the having of it,
And that you'd guide me to your sovereign's court,
Where with it I may appear a gentleman.
And if that ever my low fortune's better,
I'll pay your bounties; till then rest your debtor.

FIRST FISHERMAN Why, wilt thou tourney for the lady?

PERICLES

I'll show the virtue I have borne in arms.

FIRST FISHERMAN Why, d'ye take it, and the gods give
thee good on't.

SECOND FISHERMAN Ay, but hark you, my friend, 'twas
  we that made up this garment through the rough seams 150
  of the waters. There are certain condolements, certain
  vails. I hope, sir, if you thrive, you'll remember from
  whence you had them.

PERICLES
  Believe't, I will.
  By your furtherance I am clothed in steel,
  And spite of all the rapture of the sea
  This jewel holds his building on my arm.
  Unto thy value I will mount myself
  Upon a courser, whose delightful steps
  Shall make the gazer joy to see him tread.   160
  Only, my friend, I yet am unprovided
  Of a pair of bases.

SECOND FISHERMAN We'll sure provide. Thou shalt
  have my best gown to make thee a pair, and I'll bring
  thee to the court myself.

PERICLES
  Then honour be but a goal to my will,
  This day I'll rise, or else add ill to ill.   *Exeunt*

Enter Simonides with Lords and attendants, and Thaisa II.2

SIMONIDES
  Are the knights ready to begin the triumph?

FIRST LORD
  They are, my liege,
  And stay your coming to present themselves.

SIMONIDES
  Return them we are ready; and our daughter here,
  In honour of whose birth these triumphs are,
  Sits here like beauty's child, whom Nature gat
  For men to see and, seeing, wonder at.

THAISA

It pleaseth you, my royal father, to express
My commendations great, whose merit's less.

SIMONIDES

10 It's fit it should be so, for princes are
A model which heaven makes like to itself.
As jewels lose their glory if neglected,
So princes their renowns if not respected.
'Tis now your honour, daughter, to entertain
The labour of each knight in his device.

THAISA

Which, to preserve mine honour, I'll perform.
*The First Knight enters and passes by, his squire
presenting his shield to Thaisa*

SIMONIDES

Who is the first that doth prefer himself?

THAISA

A knight of Sparta, my renownèd father,
And the device he bears upon his shield
20 Is a black Ethiop reaching at the sun.
The word, *Lux tua vita mihi.*

SIMONIDES

He loves you well that holds his life of you.
The Second Knight passes by
Who is the second that presents himself?

THAISA

A prince of Macedon, my royal father,
And the device he bears upon his shield
Is an armed knight that's conquered by a lady.
The motto thus in Spanish, *Piu per dolcera che per forza.*
The Third Knight passes by

SIMONIDES

And with the third?

THAISA   The third of Antioch,

And his device a wreath of chivalry.
The word, *Me pompae provexit apex.*   30
  The Fourth Knight passes by

SIMONIDES

What is the fourth?

THAISA

A burning torch that's turnèd upside down.
The word, *Qui me alit me extinguit.*

SIMONIDES

Which shows that beauty hath his power and will,
Which can as well inflame as it can kill.
  The Fifth Knight passes by

THAISA

The fifth, an hand environèd with clouds,
Holding out gold that's by the touchstone tried.
The motto thus, *Sic spectanda fides.*
  The Sixth Knight, Pericles, passes by

SIMONIDES

And what's the sixth and last, the which the knight
    himself
With such a graceful courtesy delivered?   40

THAISA

He seems to be a stranger, but his present is
A withered branch that's only green at top.
The motto, *In hac spe vivo.*

SIMONIDES

A pretty moral,
From the dejected state wherein he is,
He hopes by you his fortunes yet may flourish.

FIRST LORD

He had need mean better than his outward show
Can any way speak in his just commend,
For by his rusty outside he appears
To have practised more the whipstock than the lance. 50

75

SECOND LORD

He well may be a stranger, for he comes
To an honoured triumph strangely furnishèd.

THIRD LORD

And on set purpose let his armour rust
Until this day, to scour it in the dust.

SIMONIDES

Opinion's but a fool, that makes us scan
The outward habit by the inward man.
But stay, the knights are coming.
We will withdraw into the gallery.   *Exeunt*
          (*Within*) *Great shouts, and all cry* 'The mean
          knight!'

II.3   *Enter Simonides, Thaisa, Pericles, and Knights from
          tilting, with lords, ladies, Marshal, and attendants*

SIMONIDES

Knights,
To say you're welcome were superfluous.
To place upon the volume of your deeds,
As in a title-page, your worth in arms,
Were more than you expect, or more than's fit,
Since every worth in show commends itself.
Prepare for mirth, for mirth becomes a feast.
You are princes and my guests.

THAISA (*to Pericles*)

But you, my knight and guest;
10   To whom this wreath of victory I give,
And crown you king of this day's happiness.

PERICLES

'Tis more by fortune, lady, than my merit.

SIMONIDES

Call it by what you will, the day is yours,

And here, I hope, is none that envies it.
In framing an artist, art hath thus decreed,
To make some good, but others to exceed,
And you are her laboured scholar. Come, queen o'th'
    feast –
For, daughter, so you are – here take your place.
Marshal the rest as they deserve their grace.

KNIGHTS
We are honoured much by good Simonides.   20

SIMONIDES
Your presence glads our days; honour we love,
For who hates honour hates the gods above.

MARSHAL
Sir, yonder is your place.

PERICLES   Some other is more fit.

FIRST KNIGHT
Contend not, sir, for we are gentlemen
Have neither in our hearts nor outward eyes
Envied the great nor shall the low despise.

PERICLES
You are right courteous knights.

SIMONIDES   Sit, sir, sit.
(*Aside*) By Jove, I wonder, that is king of thoughts,
These cates resist me, he but thought upon.

THAISA (*aside*)
By Juno, that is queen of marriage,   30
All viands that I eat do seem unsavoury,
Wishing him my meat. – Sure he's a gallant gentleman.

SIMONIDES
He's but a country gentleman.
He has done no more than other knights have done.
He has broken a staff or so. So let it pass.

THAISA (*aside*)
To me he seems like diamond to glass.

PERICLES (*aside*)

Yon king's to me like to my father's picture
Which tells me in what glory once he was;
Had princes sit like stars about his throne,
40   And he the sun for them to reverence.
None that beheld him but like lesser lights
Did vail their crowns to his supremacy;
Where now his son's like a glow-worm in the night,
The which hath fire in darkness, none in light;
Whereby I see that Time's the king of men;
He's both their parent and he is their grave,
And gives them what he will, not what they crave.

SIMONIDES

What, are you merry, knights?

KNIGHTS

Who can be other in this royal presence?

SIMONIDES

50   Here with a cup that's stored unto the brim,
As you do love, fill to your mistress' lips.
We drink this health to you.

KNIGHTS   We thank your grace.

SIMONIDES

Yet pause awhile.
Yon knight doth sit too melancholy,
As if the entertainment in our court
Had not a show might countervail his worth.
Note it not you, Thaisa?

THAISA

What is't to me, my father?

SIMONIDES

O, attend, my daughter:
60   Princes in this should live like gods above,
Who freely give to everyone that come to honour them.
And princes not doing so are like to gnats,

Which make a sound, but killed are wondered at.
Therefore to make his entrance more sweet,
Here, say we drink this standing-bowl of wine to him.

THAISA

Alas, my father, it befits not me
Unto a stranger knight to be so bold.
He may my proffer take for an offence,
Since men take women's gifts for impudence.

SIMONIDES

How? 70
Do as I bid you, or you'll move me else.

THAISA (*aside*)

Now, by the gods, he could not please me better.

SIMONIDES

And furthermore tell him we desire to know of him
Of whence he is, his name, and parentage.

THAISA

The King my father, sir, has drunk to you.

PERICLES

I thank him.

THAISA

Wishing it so much blood unto your life.

PERICLES

I thank both him and you, and pledge him freely.

THAISA

And further he desires to know of you
Of whence you are, your name, and parentage. 80

PERICLES

A gentleman of Tyre, my name Pericles,
My education been in arts and arms,
Who, looking for adventures in the world,
Was by the rough seas reft of ships and men,
And after shipwreck driven upon this shore.

79

THAISA

He thanks your grace, names himself Pericles,
A gentleman of Tyre,
Who only by misfortune of the seas,
Bereft of ships and men, cast on this shore.

SIMONIDES

90 Now, by the gods, I pity his misfortune
And will awake him from his melancholy.
Come, gentlemen, we sit too long on trifles,
And waste the time which looks for other revels.
Even in your armours, as you are addressed,
Will well become a soldiers' dance.
I will not have excuse with saying this:
Loud music is too harsh for ladies' heads,
Since they love men in arms as well as beds.
    They dance
So, this was well asked, 'twas so well performed.
100 Come, sir, here's a lady that wants breathing too,
And I have heard you knights of Tyre
Are excellent in making ladies trip,
And that their measures are as excellent.

PERICLES

In those that practise them they are, my lord.

SIMONIDES

O, that's as much as you would be denied
Of your fair courtesy.
    They dance
                        Unclasp, unclasp!
Thanks, gentlemen, to all. All have done well,
(*to Pericles*) But you the best. – Pages and lights, to
    conduct
These knights unto their several lodgings. –
110 Yours, sir, we have given order be next our own.

PERICLES

I am at your grace's pleasure.

SIMONIDES

Princes, it is too late to talk of love,
And that's the mark I know you level at.
Therefore each one betake him to his rest;
Tomorrow all for speeding do their best.   *Exeunt*

Enter Helicanus and Escanes   II.4

HELICANUS

No, Escanes, know this of me,
Antiochus from incest lived not free.
For which the most high gods not minding longer
To withhold the vengeance that they had in store,
Due to this heinous capital offence,
Even in the height and pride of all his glory,
When he was seated in a chariot
Of an inestimable value, and his daughter with him,
A fire from heaven came and shrivelled up
Their bodies even to loathing; for they so stunk   10
That all those eyes adored them ere their fall
Scorn now their hand should give them burial.

ESCANES

'Twas very strange.

HELICANUS   And yet but justice, for though
This king were great, his greatness was no guard
To bar heaven's shaft, but sin had his reward.

ESCANES

'Tis very true.

Enter two or three Lords

FIRST LORD

See, not a man in private conference
Or council has respect with him but he.

SECOND LORD

It shall no longer grieve without reproof.

THIRD LORD

20   And cursed be he that will not second it.

FIRST LORD

Follow me then. Lord Helicane, a word.

HELICANUS

With me? And welcome. Happy day, my lords.

FIRST LORD

Know that our griefs are risen to the top,
And now at length they overflow their banks.

HELICANUS

Your griefs? For what? Wrong not your prince you
love.

FIRST LORD

Wrong not yourself then, noble Helicane,
But if the prince do live, let us salute him
And know what ground's made happy by his breath.
If in the world he live, we'll seek him out;
30   If in his grave he rest, we'll find him there;
And be resolved he lives to govern us,
Or dead, give's cause to mourn his funeral
And leave us to our free election.

SECOND LORD

Whose death indeed's the strongest in our censure,
And knowing this: kingdoms without a head,
Like goodly buildings left without a roof,
Soon fall to ruin, your noble self,
That best know how to rule and how to reign,
We thus submit unto, our sovereign.

ALL

40   Live, noble Helicane!

HELICANUS

Try honour's cause; forbear your suffrages.
If that you love Prince Pericles, forbear.

Take I your wish, I leap into the seas,
Where's hourly trouble, for a minute's ease.
A twelvemonth longer let me entreat you
Further to bear the absence of your king;
If in which time expired he not return,
I shall with agèd patience bear your yoke.
But if I cannot win you to this love,
Go search like nobles, like noble subjects,   50
And in your search spend your adventurous worth.
Whom if you find, and win unto return,
You shall like diamonds sit about his crown.

FIRST LORD
To wisdom he's a fool that will not yield,
And since Lord Helicane enjoineth us,
We with our travels will endeavour it.

HELICANUS
Then you love us, we you, and we'll clasp hands.
When peers thus knit, a kingdom ever stands.   *Exeunt*

Enter Simonides, reading of a letter, at one door. The   II.5
Knights meet him

FIRST KNIGHT
Good morrow to the good Simonides.

SIMONIDES
Knights, from my daughter this I let you know,
That for this twelvemonth she'll not undertake
A married life.
Her reason to herself is only known,
Which from her by no means can I get.

SECOND KNIGHT
May we not get access to her, my lord?

SIMONIDES
Faith, by no means. She hath so strictly

Tied her to her chamber, that 'tis impossible.
10 One twelve moons more she'll wear Diana's livery.
This by the eye of Cynthia hath she vowed
And on her virgin honour will not break it.

THIRD KNIGHT

Loath to bid farewell, we take our leaves. *Exeunt Knights*

SIMONIDES

So, they are well dispatched.
Now to my daughter's letter.
She tells me here she'll wed the stranger knight,
Or never more to view nor day nor light.
'Tis well, mistress, your choice agrees with mine.
I like that well. Nay, how absolute she's in't,
20 Not minding whether I dislike or no.
Well, I do commend her choice,
And will no longer have it be delayed.
Soft, here he comes; I must dissemble it.
     Enter Pericles

PERICLES

All fortune to the good Simonides!

SIMONIDES

To you as much, sir. I am beholding to you
For your sweet music this last night. I do
Protest my ears were never better fed
With such delightful, pleasing harmony.

PERICLES

It is your grace's pleasure to commend,
Not my desert.

30 SIMONIDES   Sir, you are music's master.

PERICLES

The worst of all her scholars, my good lord.

SIMONIDES

Let me ask you one thing. What do you think
Of my daughter, sir?

PERICLES   A most virtuous princess.

SIMONIDES

  And she is fair too, is she not?

PERICLES

  As a fair day in summer, wondrous fair.

SIMONIDES

  Sir, my daughter thinks very well of you;

  Ay, so well, that you must be her master,

  And she will be your scholar. Therefore, look to it.

PERICLES

  I am unworthy for her schoolmaster.

SIMONIDES

  She thinks not so; peruse this writing else.   40

PERICLES (*aside*)

  What's here?

  A letter that she loves the knight of Tyre!

  'Tis the King's subtlety to have my life. –

  O, seek not to entrap me, gracious lord,

  A stranger and distressèd gentleman,

  That never aimed so high to love your daughter,

  But bent all offices to honour her.

SIMONIDES

  Thou hast bewitched my daughter,

  And thou art a villain.

PERICLES   By the gods, I have not.

  Never did thought of mine levy offence,   50

  Nor never did my actions yet commence

  A deed might gain her love or your displeasure.

SIMONIDES

  Traitor, thou liest.

PERICLES   Traitor!

SIMONIDES   Ay, traitor,

  [That thus disguised art stolen into my court,

  With the witchcraft of thy actions to bewitch

The yielding spirit of my tender child.]

PERICLES

Even in his throat, unless it be the King,
That calls me traitor, I return the lie.

SIMONIDES (*aside*)

Now, by the gods, I do applaud his courage.

PERICLES

60 My actions are as noble as my thoughts,
That never relished of a base descent.
I came unto your court for honour's cause,
And not to be a rebel to her state.
And he that otherwise accounts of me,
This sword shall prove he's honour's enemy.

SIMONIDES

No?
Here comes my daughter. She can witness it.

> *Enter Thaisa*

PERICLES

Then, as you are as virtuous as fair,
Resolve your angry father if my tongue
70 Did e'er solicit, or my hand subscribe
To any syllable that made love to you.

THAISA

Why, sir, say if you had, who takes offence
At that would make me glad?

SIMONIDES

Yea, mistress, are you so peremptory?
(*Aside*) I am glad on't with all my heart. –
I'll tame you, I'll bring you in subjection.
Will you, not having my consent,
Bestow your love and your affections
Upon a stranger? (*aside*) who, for aught I know,
80 May be, nor can I think the contrary,
As great in blood as I myself –

86

[A straggling Theseus born we know not where?]
Therefore, hear you, mistress, either frame
Your will to mine – and you, sir, hear you,
Either be ruled by me, or I'll make you –
Man and wife.
Nay, come, your hands and lips must seal it too.
And being joined, I'll thus your hopes destroy,
And for further grief – God give you joy!
What, are you both pleased?

THAISA   Yes, if you love me, sir? 90

PERICLES
Even as my life my blood that fosters it.

SIMONIDES
What, are you both agreed?

PERICLES *and* THAISA
Yes, if't please your majesty.

SIMONIDES
It pleaseth me so well that I will see you wed;
And then, with what haste you can, get you to bed.

                                        Exeunt

✳

III CHORUS

Enter Gower

GOWER
Now sleep y-slackèd hath the rout,
No din but snores about the house,
Made louder by the o'erfed breast
Of this most pompous marriage-feast.
The cat, with eyne of burning coal,
Now couches 'fore the mouse's hole,   *cat/mouse*
And crickets sing at the oven's mouth,

All the blither for their drouth.
Hymen hath brought the bride to bed,
Where, by the loss of maidenhead,
A babe is moulded. Be attent,
And time that is so briefly spent
With your fine fancies quaintly eche.
What's dumb in show, I'll plain with speech.

Dumb show:
Enter Pericles and Simonides at one door with
attendants. A messenger meets them, kneels, and gives
Pericles a letter. Pericles shows it Simonides; the
lords kneel to him. Then enter Thaisa with child, with
Lychorida, a nurse. The King shows her the letter;
she rejoices. She and Pericles take leave of her father
and depart with Lychorida. The rest go out

By many a dern and painful perch
Of Pericles the careful search,
By the four opposing coigns
Which the world together joins,
Is made with all due diligence
That horse and sail and high expense
Can stead the quest. At last from Tyre,
Fame answering the most strange inquire,
To th'court of King Simonides
Are letters brought, the tenor these:
Antiochus and his daughter dead,
The men of Tyrus on the head
Of Helicanus would set on
The crown of Tyre, but he will none.
The mutiny he there hastes t'oppress;
Says to 'em, if King Pericles
Come not home in twice six moons,
He, obedient to their dooms,
Will take the crown. The sum of this,

Brought hither to Pentapolis,
Y-ravishèd the regions round,
And everyone with claps can sound
'Our heir-apparent is a king!
Who dreamed, who thought of such a thing?'
Brief, he must hence depart to Tyre.
His queen with child makes her desire –   40
Which who shall cross? – along to go.
Omit we all their dole and woe.
Lychorida her nurse she takes,
And so to sea. Their vessel shakes
On Neptune's billow; half the flood
Hath their keel cut; but fortune's mood
Varies again; the grisled north
Disgorges such a tempest forth
That, as a duck for life that dives,
So up and down the poor ship drives.   50
The lady shrieks and, well-a-near,
Does fall in travail with her fear.
And what ensues in this fell storm
Shall for itself itself perform.
I nill relate, action may
Conveniently the rest convey,
Which might not what by me is told.
In your imagination hold
This stage the ship, upon whose deck
The sea-tossed Pericles appears to speak.   *Exit* 60

Enter Pericles a-shipboard   III.1

PERICLES
The god of this great vast rebuke these surges,
Which wash both heaven and hell. And thou that hast
Upon the winds command, bind them in brass,

Having called them from the deep! O, still
Thy deafening, dreadful thunders, gently quench
Thy nimble, sulphurous flashes! O, how, Lychorida,
How does my queen? Thou storm, venomously
Wilt thou spit all thyself? The seaman's whistle
Is as a whisper in the ears of death,
10 Unheard. Lychorida! Lucina, O
Divinest patroness and midwife gentle
To those that cry by night, convey thy deity
Aboard our dancing boat, make swift the pangs
Of my queen's travails! Now, Lychorida!

Enter Lychorida with a baby

LYCHORIDA
Here is a thing too young for such a place,
Who if it had conceit would die as I
Am like to do. Take in your arms this piece
Of your dead queen.

PERICLES   How? How, Lychorida?

LYCHORIDA
Patience, good sir, do not assist the storm.
20 Here's all that is left living of your queen,
A little daughter; for the sake of it,
Be manly and take comfort.

PERICLES   O you gods!
Why do you make us love your goodly gifts
And snatch them straight away? We here below
Recall not what we give, and therein may
Use honour with you.

LYCHORIDA   Patience, good sir,
Even for this charge.

PERICLES   Now, mild may be thy life!
For a more blusterous birth had never babe;
Quiet and gentle thy conditions! for
30 Thou art the rudeliest welcome to this world

That ever was prince's child. Happy what follows!
Thou hast as chiding a nativity
As fire, air, water, earth, and heaven can make
To herald thee from the womb. [Poor inch of nature!]
Even at the first thy loss is more than can
Thy portage quit, with all thou canst find here.
Now the good gods throw their best eyes upon't.

Enter two Sailors

FIRST SAILOR What courage, sir? God save you!

PERICLES
Courage enough. I do not fear the flaw;   40
It hath done to me the worst. Yet for the love
Of this poor infant, this fresh new seafarer,
I would it would be quiet.

FIRST SAILOR Slack the bolins there! – Thou wilt not,
wilt thou? Blow and split thyself.

SECOND SAILOR But sea-room, an the brine and cloudy
billow kiss the moon, I care not.

FIRST SAILOR Sir, your queen must overboard. The sea
works high, the wind is loud, and will not lie till the
ship be cleared of the dead.

PERICLES That's your superstition.   50

FIRST SAILOR Pardon us, sir; with us at sea it hath been
still observed, and we are strong in custom. Therefore
briefly yield 'er, for she must overboard straight.

PERICLES
As you think meet. Most wretched queen!

LYCHORIDA Here she lies, sir.

She reveals the body of Thaisa

PERICLES
A terrible childbed hast thou had, my dear;
No light, no fire; th'unfriendly elements
Forgot thee utterly. Nor have I time
To give thee hallowed to thy grave, but straight

60 Must cast thee, scarcely coffined, in the ooze,
Where, for a monument upon thy bones,
And e'er-remaining lamps, the belching whale
And humming water must o'erwhelm thy corpse,
Lying with simple shells. O Lychorida,
Bid Nestor bring me spices, ink and paper,
My casket and my jewels. And bid Nicander
Bring me the satin coffer. Lay the babe
Upon the pillow. Hie thee, whiles I say
A priestly farewell to her. Suddenly, woman.

Exit Lychorida

70 SECOND SAILOR Sir, we have a chest beneath the
hatches, caulked and bitumed ready.

PERICLES
I thank thee. Mariner, say, what coast is this?

FIRST SAILOR We are near Tarsus.

PERICLES
Thither, gentle mariner,
Alter thy course for Tyre. When canst thou reach it?

FIRST SAILOR By break of day, if the wind cease.

PERICLES
O, make for Tarsus!
There will I visit Cleon, for the babe
Cannot hold out to Tyrus. There I'll leave it

80 At careful nursing. Go thy ways, good mariner;
I'll bring the body presently.   *Exeunt*

III.2   *Enter Lord Cerimon and two Servants*

CERIMON Philemon, ho!
        Enter Philemon

PHILEMON Doth my lord call?

CERIMON
Get fire and meat for these poor men.

92

'T'as been a turbulent and stormy night. *Exit Philemon*

FIRST SERVANT
    I have been in many, but such a night as this
    Till now I ne'er endured.

CERIMON (*to First Servant*)
    Your master will be dead ere you return.
    There's nothing can be ministered to nature
    That can recover him. (*To Second Servant*) Give this to
        the pothecary
    And tell me how it works.   *Exeunt Servants*
        Enter two Gentlemen

FIRST GENTLEMAN   Good morrow.   10
SECOND GENTLEMAN
    Good morrow to your lordship.

CERIMON   Gentlemen,
    Why do you stir so early?

FIRST GENTLEMAN   Sir,
    Our lodgings, standing bleak upon the sea,
    Shook as the earth did quake.
    The very principals did seem to rend
    And all to topple. Pure surprise and fear
    Made me to quit the house.

SECOND GENTLEMAN
    That is the cause we trouble you so early;
    'Tis not our husbandry.

CERIMON   O, you say well.

FIRST GENTLEMAN
    But I much marvel that your lordship, having   20
    Rich tire about you, should at these early hours
    Shake off the golden slumber of repose.
    'Tis most strange
    Nature should be so conversant with pain,
    Being thereto not compelled.

CERIMON   I held it ever

Virtue and cunning were endowments greater
Than nobleness and riches. Careless heirs
May the two latter darken and expend,
But immortality attends the former,
30   Making a man a god. 'Tis known I ever
Have studied physic, through which secret art,
By turning o'er authorities, I have,
Together with my practice, made familiar
To me and to my aid the blest infusions
That dwells in vegetives, in metals, stones;
And I can speak of the disturbances
That nature works, and of her cures; which doth give
    me
A more content in course of true delight
Than to be thirsty after tottering honour,
40   Or tie my pleasure up in silken bags,
To please the fool and death.

SECOND GENTLEMAN   Your honour has
Through Ephesus poured forth your charity,
And hundreds call themselves your creatures, who
By you have been restored. And not your knowledge,
Your personal pain, but even your purse, still open,
Hath built Lord Cerimon such strong renown
As time shall never –

Enter two or three with a chest

FIRST SERVANT
So, lift there!

CERIMON   What's that?

FIRST SERVANT   Sir, even now
Did the sea toss up upon our shore this chest.
'Tis of some wreck.

50 CERIMON   Set't down, let's look upon't.

SECOND GENTLEMAN
'Tis like a coffin, sir.

CERIMON   Whate'er it be,
  'Tis wondrous heavy. Wrench it open straight.
  If the sea's stomach be o'ercharged with gold,
  'Tis a good constraint of fortune it belches upon us.

SECOND GENTLEMAN
  'Tis so, my lord.

CERIMON   How close 'tis caulked and bitumed!
  Did the sea cast it up?

FIRST SERVANT
  I never saw so huge a billow, sir,
  As tossed it upon shore.

CERIMON   Wrench it open. Soft!
  It smells most sweetly in my sense.

SECOND GENTLEMAN   A delicate odour.

CERIMON
  As ever hit my nostril. So, up with it!   60
  O you most potent gods, what's here? A corse?

SECOND GENTLEMAN
  Most strange!

CERIMON
  Shrouded in cloth of state, balmed and entreasured
  With full bags of spices! A passport too!
  Apollo, perfect me in the characters!

    He reads the scroll

  Here I give to understand,
  If e'er this coffin drives a-land,
  I, King Pericles, have lost
  This queen, worth all our mundane cost.
  Who finds her, give her burying;   70
  She was the daughter of a king.
  Besides this treasure for a fee,
  The gods requite his charity.

  If thou livest, Pericles, thou hast a heart

That ever cracks for woe. This chanced tonight.

SECOND GENTLEMAN
Most likely, sir.

CERIMON   Nay, certainly tonight,
For look how fresh she looks. They were too rough
That threw her in the sea. Make a fire within.
Fetch hither all my boxes in my closet. *Exit a servant*
80 Death may usurp on nature many hours,
And yet the fire of life kindle again
The o'erpressed spirits. [I have read
Of some Egyptians who after four hours' death
Have raised impoverished bodies, like to this,
Unto their former health.]
        Enter one with napkins and fire
Well said, well said, the fire and cloths.
The rough and woeful music that we have,
Cause it to sound, beseech you.
        Music plays while Cerimon attends to Thaisa
The viol once more! How thou stirrest, thou block!
The music there!
        Music again
90   I pray you give her air.
Gentlemen, this queen will live!
Nature awakes. A warmth breathes out of her.
She hath not been entranced above five hours.
See how she 'gins to blow into life's flower again.

FIRST GENTLEMAN
The heavens, through you, increase our wonder, and
Sets up your fame for ever.

CERIMON   She is alive. Behold,
Her eyelids, cases to those heavenly jewels
Which Pericles hath lost, begin to part
Their fringes of bright gold. The diamonds
100 Of a most praisèd water doth appear

To make the world twice rich. Live,
And make us weep to hear your fate, fair creature,
Rare as you seem to be.

    She moves

THAISA   O dear Diana!
Where am I? Where's my lord? What world is this?

SECOND GENTLEMAN
Is not this strange?

FIRST GENTLEMAN Most rare.

CERIMON
Hush, my gentle neighbours.
Lend me your hands. To the next chamber bear her.
Get linen. Now this matter must be looked to,
For her relapse is mortal. Come, come;
And Aesculapius guide us.   110

                      They carry her away. Exeunt

    Enter Pericles at Tarsus with Cleon and Dionyza,   III.3
    and Lychorida with the baby in her arms

PERICLES
Most honoured Cleon, I must needs be gone.
My twelve months are expired, and Tyrus stands
In a litigious peace. You and your lady
Take from my heart all thankfulness. The gods
Make up the rest upon you!

CLEON   Your shakes of fortune,
Though they haunt you mortally, yet glance
Full wonderingly on us.

DIONYZA   O, your sweet queen!
That the strict fates had pleased you had brought her
      hither,
To have blessed mine eyes with her.

PERICLES   We cannot but obey

10 The powers above us. Could I rage and roar
As doth the sea she lies in, yet the end
Must be as 'tis. My gentle babe Marina,
Whom, for she was born at sea, I have named so,
Here I charge your charity withal, leaving her
The infant of your care, beseeching you
To give her princely training, that she may
Be mannered as she is born.

CLEON   Fear not, my lord, but think
Your grace, that fed my country with your corn,
For which the people's prayers still fall upon you,
20 Must in your child be thought on. If neglection
Should therein make me vile, the common body
By you relieved would force me to my duty.
But if to that my nature need a spur,
The gods revenge it upon me and mine
To the end of generation.

PERICLES   I believe you.
Your honour and your goodness teach me to't
Without your vows. Till she be married, madam,
By bright Diana, whom we honour, all
Unscissored shall this hair of mine remain,
30 Though I show will in't. So I take my leave.
Good madam, make me blessèd in your care
In bringing up my child.

DIONYZA   I have one myself,
Who shall not be more dear to my respect
Than yours, my lord.

PERICLES   Madam, my thanks and prayers.

CLEON
We'll bring your grace e'en to the edge o'th'shore,
Then give you up to the masked Neptune, and
The gentlest winds of heaven.

PERICLES   I will embrace

Your offer. Come, dearest madam. O, no tears,
Lychorida, no tears.
Look to your little mistress, on whose grace   40
You may depend hereafter. Come, my lord. *Exeunt*

Enter Cerimon and Thaisa   III.4

CERIMON

Madam, this letter, and some certain jewels,
Lay with you in your coffer, which are
At your command. Know you the character?

THAISA

It is my lord's.
That I was shipped at sea I well remember,
Even on my bearing time. But whether there
Delivered, by the holy gods,
I cannot rightly say. But since King Pericles,
My wedded lord, I ne'er shall see again,
A vestal livery will I take me to,   10
And never more have joy.

CERIMON

Madam, if this you purpose as ye speak,
Diana's temple is not distant far,
Where you may abide till your date expire.
Moreover, if you please, a niece of mine
Shall there attend you.

THAISA

My recompense is thanks, that's all;
Yet my good will is great, though the gift small.
                                            Exeunt

*

Enter Gower

GOWER

    Imagine Pericles arrived at Tyre,
    Welcomed and settled to his own desire.
    His woeful queen we leave at Ephesus,
    Unto Diana there's a votaress.
    Now to Marina bend your mind,
    Whom our fast-growing scene must find
    At Tarsus, and by Cleon trained
    In music's letters; who hath gained
    Of education all the grace,
10   Which makes her both the heart and place
    Of general wonder. But, alack,
    That monster envy, oft the wrack
    Of earnèd praise, Marina's life
    Seeks to take off by treason's knife.
    And in this kind, our Cleon hath
    One daughter and a full-grown wench,
    Even ripe for marriage-rite. This maid
    Hight Philoten, and it is said
    For certain in our story she
20   Would ever with Marina be;
    Be't when she weaved the sleded silk
    With fingers long, small, white as milk;
    Or when she would with sharp needle wound
    The cambric, which she made more sound
    By hurting it; or when to th'lute
    She sung, and made the night-bird mute,
    That still records with moan; or when
    She would with rich and constant pen
    Vail to her mistress Dian. Still

This Philoten contends in skill   30
With absolute Marina. So
With dove of Paphos might the crow
Vie feathers white. Marina gets
All praises, which are paid as debts,
And not as given. This so darks
In Philoten all graceful marks
That Cleon's wife, with envy rare,
A present murderer does prepare
For good Marina, that her daughter
Might stand peerless by this slaughter.   40
The sooner her vile thoughts to stead,
Lychorida, our nurse, is dead,
And cursèd Dionyza hath
The pregnant instrument of wrath
Prest for this blow. The unborn event
I do commend to your content.
Only I carried wingèd time
Post on the lame feet of my rhyme,
Which never could I so convey
Unless your thoughts went on my way.   50
Dionyza does appear
With Leonine, a murderer.   *Exit*

Enter Dionyza with Leonine   IV.1
DIONYZA
Thy oath remember. Thou hast sworn to do't.
'Tis but a blow, which never shall be known.
Thou canst not do a thing in the world so soon
To yield thee so much profit. Let not conscience,
Which is but cold, inflaming love in thy bosom,
Inflame too nicely; nor let pity, which
Even women have cast off, melt thee, but be

A soldier to thy purpose.

LEONINE   I will do't –
But yet she is a goodly creature.

DIONYZA

10   The fitter then the gods should have her.
   Here she comes weeping for her only mistress' death.
   Thou art resolved?

LEONINE   I am resolved.

Enter Marina with a basket of flowers

MARINA

No, I will rob Tellus of her weed
To strew thy green with flowers. The yellows, blues,
The purple violets, and marigolds
Shall as a carpet hang upon thy grave
While summer days doth last. Ay me, poor maid,
Born in a tempest when my mother died,
This world to me is as a lasting storm,

20 Whirring me from my friends.

DIONYZA

How now, Marina? Why do you keep alone?
How chance my daughter is not with you?
Do not consume your blood with sorrowing;
Have you a nurse of me. Lord, how your favour's
Changed with this unprofitable woe!
Come, give me your flowers. On the sea-margent
Walk with Leonine. The air is quick there,
And it pierces and sharpens the stomach.
Come, Leonine. Take her by the arm, walk with her.

MARINA

30 No, I pray you. I'll not bereave you of your servant.

DIONYZA

Come, come.
I love the King your father and yourself
With more than foreign heart. We every day

Expect him here. When he shall come and find
Our paragon to all reports thus blasted,
He will repent the breadth of his great voyage,
Blame both my lord and me that we have taken
No care to your best courses. Go, I pray you.
Walk and be cheerful once again. Reserve
That excellent complexion which did steal   40
The eyes of young and old. Care not for me;
I can go home alone.

MARINA   Well, I will go,
But yet I have no desire to it.

DIONYZA
Come, come, I know 'tis good for you.
Walk half an hour, Leonine, at the least.
Remember what I have said.

LEONINE
I warrant you, madam.

DIONYZA
I'll leave you, my sweet lady, for a while.
Pray walk softly, do not heat your blood.
What! I must have care of you.

MARINA   My thanks, sweet madam. 50

Exit Dionyza

Is this wind westerly that blows?

LEONINE   South-west.

MARINA
When I was born the wind was north.

LEONINE   Was't so?

MARINA
My father, as nurse says, did never fear,
But cried 'Good seamen!' to the sailors, galling
His kingly hands haling ropes,
And, clasping to the mast, endured a sea
That almost burst the deck.

LEONINE
When was this?

MARINA
When I was born.

60   Never was waves nor wind more violent,
And from the ladder-tackle washes off
A canvas-climber. 'Ha!' says one, 'wolt out?'
And with a dropping industry they skip
From stem to stern. The boatswain whistles, and
The master calls and trebles their confusion.

LEONINE
Come, say your prayers.

MARINA
What mean you?

LEONINE
If you require a little space for prayer,
I grant it. Pray; but be not tedious, for
70   The gods are quick of ear, and I am sworn
To do my work with haste.

MARINA   Why will you kill me?

LEONINE
To satisfy my lady.

MARINA
Why would she have me killed?
Now, as I can remember, by my troth,
I never did her hurt in all my life.
I never spake bad word nor did ill turn
To any living creature. Believe me, law,
I never killed a mouse, nor hurt a fly.
I trod upon a worm against my will,
80   But I wept for't. How have I offended,
Wherein my death might yield her any profit,
Or my life imply her any danger?

LEONINE
My commission
Is not to reason of the deed, but do't.
MARINA
You will not do't for all the world, I hope.
You are well-favoured, and your looks foreshow
You have a gentle heart. I saw you lately
When you caught hurt in parting two that fought.
Good sooth, it showed well in you. Do so now.
Your lady seeks my life; come you between,   90
And save poor me, the weaker.
LEONINE   I am sworn,
And will dispatch.
          He seizes her
          Enter Pirates
FIRST PIRATE Hold, villain!   *Leonine runs away*
SECOND PIRATE A prize, a prize!
THIRD PIRATE Half-part, mates, half-part. Come, let's
have her aboard suddenly.
                    Exeunt Pirates, carrying off Marina
          Enter Leonine
LEONINE
These roguing thieves serve the great pirate Valdes,
And they have seized Marina. Let her go.
There's no hope she will return. I'll swear she's dead,
And thrown into the sea. But I'll see further.   100
Perhaps they will but please themselves upon her,
Not carry her aboard. If she remain,
Whom they have ravished must by me be slain.
                                        Exit

          Enter the three Bawds   IV.2
PANDER Boult!

105

BOULT Sir?

PANDER Search the market narrowly. Mytilene is full of
gallants. We lost too much money this mart by being too
wenchless.

BAWD We were never so much out of creatures. We have
but poor three, and they can do no more than they can
do. And they with continual action are even as good as
rotten.

10 PANDER Therefore let's have fresh ones, whate'er we pay
for them. If there be not a conscience to be used in every
trade, we shall never prosper.

BAWD Thou sayst true. 'Tis not our bringing up of poor
bastards – as I think, I have brought up some eleven –

BOULT Ay, to eleven, and brought them down again. But
shall I search the market?

BAWD What else, man? The stuff we have, a strong wind
will blow it to pieces, they are so pitifully sodden.

PANDER Thou sayst true, there's two unwholesome, o'
20 conscience. The poor Transylvanian is dead that lay
with the little baggage.

BOULT Ay, she quickly pooped him; she made him roast
meat for worms. But I'll go search the market. *Exit*

PANDER Three or four thousand chequins were as pretty
a proportion to live quietly, and so give over.

BAWD Why to give over, I pray you? Is it a shame to get
when we are old?

PANDER O, our credit comes not in like the commodity,
nor the commodity wages not with the danger. There-
30 fore, if in our youths we could pick up some pretty
estate, 'twere not amiss to keep our door hatched.
Besides, the sore terms we stand upon with the gods will
be strong with us for giving o'er.

BAWD Come, other sorts offend as well as we.

PANDER As well as we? Ay, and better too; we offend

worse. Neither is our profession any trade; it's no
calling. But here comes Boult.

Enter Boult with the Pirates and Marina

BOULT Come your ways, my masters. You say she's a
virgin?

FIRST PIRATE O, sir, we doubt it not.   40

BOULT Master, I have gone through for this piece you see.
If you like her, so. If not, I have lost my earnest.

BAWD Boult, has she any qualities?

BOULT She has a good face, speaks well, and has excellent
good clothes. There's no farther necessity of qualities
can make her be refused.

BAWD What's her price, Boult?

BOULT I cannot be bated one doit of a thousand pieces.

PANDER Well, follow me, my masters; you shall have
your money presently. Wife, take her in. Instruct her   50
what she has to do, that she may not be raw in her
entertainment.   *Exeunt Pander and Pirates*

BAWD Boult, take you the marks of her, the colour of her
hair, complexion, height, her age, with warrant of her
virginity, and cry 'He that will give most shall have her
first.' Such a maidenhead were no cheap thing, if men
were as they have been. Get this done as I command
you.

BOULT Performance shall follow.   *Exit*

MARINA

Alack that Leonine was so slack, so slow!   60
He should have struck, not spoke. Or that these pirates,
Not enough barbarous, had not o'erboard
Thrown me for to seek my mother!

BAWD Why lament you, pretty one?

MARINA That I am pretty.

BAWD Come, the gods have done their part in you.

MARINA I accuse them not.

BAWD You are light into my hands, where you are like to live.

MARINA

70 The more my fault

To 'scape his hands where I was like to die.

BAWD Ay, and you shall live in pleasure.

MARINA No.

BAWD Yes, indeed shall you, and taste gentlemen of all fashions. You shall fare well. You shall have the difference of all complexions. What, do you stop your ears?

MARINA Are you a woman?

BAWD What would you have me be, an I be not a woman?

80 MARINA An honest woman, or not a woman.

BAWD Marry, whip the gosling. I think I shall have something to do with you. Come, you're a young foolish sapling, and must be bowed as I would have you.

MARINA The gods defend me!

BAWD If it please the gods to defend you by men, then men must comfort you, men must feed you, men stir you up. Boult's returned.

Enter Boult

Now, sir, hast thou cried her through the market?

BOULT I have cried her almost to the number of her hairs.

90 I have drawn her picture with my voice.

BAWD And I prithee tell me, how dost thou find the inclination of the people, especially of the younger sort?

BOULT Faith, they listened to me as they would have hearkened to their father's testament. There was a Spaniard's mouth watered, and he went to bed to her very description.

BAWD We shall have him here tomorrow with his best ruff on.

BOULT Tonight, tonight. But, mistress, do you know the French knight, that cowers i'the hams? 100

BAWD Who, Monsieur Veroles?

BOULT Ay, he. He offered to cut a caper at the proclamation, but he made a groan at it, and swore he would see her tomorrow.

BAWD Well, well, as for him, he brought his disease hither; here he does but repair it. I know he will come in our shadow to scatter his crowns of the sun.

BOULT Well, if we had of every nation a traveller, we should lodge them with this sign.

BAWD (*to Marina*) Pray you, come hither awhile. You 110 have fortunes coming upon you. Mark me. You must seem to do that fearfully which you commit willingly; despise profit where you have most gain. To weep that you live as ye do makes pity in your lovers. Seldom but that pity begets you a good opinion, and that opinion a mere profit.

MARINA I understand you not.

BOULT O, take her home, mistress, take her home. These blushes of hers must be quenched with some present practice. 120

BAWD Thou sayst true, i'faith, so they must, for your bride goes to that with shame which is her way to go with warrant.

BOULT Faith, some do and some do not. But, mistress, if I have bargained for the joint –

BAWD Thou mayst cut a morsel off the spit.

BOULT I may so.

BAWD Who should deny it? Come, young one. I like the manner of your garments well.

BOULT Ay, by my faith, they shall not be changed yet. 130

BAWD Boult, spend thou that in the town. Report what a sojourner we have. You'll lose nothing by custom.

When nature framed this piece, she meant thee a good
turn. Therefore say what a paragon she is, and thou hast
the harvest out of thine own report.

BOULT I warrant you, mistress, thunder shall not so awake
the beds of eels as my giving out her beauty stirs up the
lewdly inclined. I'll bring home some tonight.

BAWD (*to Marina*) Come your ways. Follow me.

MARINA

140 If fires be hot, knives sharp, or waters deep,
Untied I still my virgin knot will keep.
Diana, aid my purpose!

BAWD What have we to do with Diana? Pray you will you
go with us?   *Exeunt*

IV.3   *Enter Cleon and Dionyza*

DIONYZA
Why are you foolish? Can it be undone?

CLEON
O Dionyza, such a piece of slaughter
The sun and moon ne'er looked upon.

DIONYZA
I think you'll turn a child again.

CLEON
Were I chief lord of all this spacious world,
I'd give it to undo the deed. A lady
Much less in blood than virtue, yet a princess
To equal any single crown o'th'earth
I'th'justice of compare. O villain Leonine!

10 Whom thou hast poisoned too.
If thou hadst drunk to him, 't had been a kindness
Becoming well thy fact. What canst thou say
When noble Pericles shall demand his child?

DIONYZA

    That she is dead. Nurses are not the Fates.

    To foster is not ever to preserve.

    She died at night. I'll say so. Who can cross it?

    Unless you play the impious innocent

    And, for an honest attribute, cry out

    'She died by foul play.'

CLEON   O, go to! Well, well,

    Of all the faults beneath the heavens, the gods   20

    Do like this worst.

DIONYZA   Be one of those that thinks

    The petty wrens of Tarsus will fly hence

    And open this to Pericles. I do shame

    To think of what a noble strain you are,

    And of how coward a spirit.

CLEON   To such proceeding

    Whoever but his approbation added,

    Though not his prime consent, he did not flow

    From honourable courses.

DIONYZA   Be it so, then.

    Yet none does know but you how she came dead,

    Nor none can know, Leonine being gone.   30

    She did distain my child, and stood between

    Her and her fortunes. None would look on her,

    But cast their gazes on Marina's face,

    Whilst ours was blurted at, and held a malkin,

    Not worth the time of day. It pierced me through.

    And though you call my course unnatural,

    You not your child well loving, yet I find

    It greets me as an enterprise of kindness

    Performed to your sole daughter.

CLEON   Heavens forgive it!

DIONYZA

    And as for Pericles,   40

What should he say? We wept after her hearse,
And yet we mourn. Her monument
Is almost finished, and her epitaphs
In glittering golden characters express
A general praise to her, and care in us
At whose expense 'tis done.

CLEON   Thou art like the harpy,
Which, to betray, dost with thine angel's face
Seize with thine eagle's talons.

DIONYZA
Ye are like one that superstitiously
50 Do swear to th'gods that winter kills the flies.
But yet I know you'll do as I advise.   *Exeunt*

IV.4   *Enter Gower*

GOWER
Thus time we waste, and long leagues make short,
Sail seas in cockles, have and wish but for't,
Making to take your imagination
From bourn to bourn, region to region.
By you being pardoned, we commit no crime
To use one language in each several clime
Where our scene seems to live. I do beseech you
To learn of me, who stand i'th'gaps to teach you
The stages of our story. Pericles
10 Is now again thwarting the wayward seas,
Attended on by many a lord and knight,
To see his daughter, all his life's delight.
Old Helicanus goes along. Behind
Is left to govern it, you bear in mind,
Old Escanes, whom Helicanus late
Advanced in time to great and high estate.
Well-sailing ships and bounteous winds have brought

This king to Tarsus – think his pilot thought;
So with his steerage shall your thoughts grow on –
To fetch his daughter home, who first is gone.   20
Like motes and shadows see them move awhile;
Your ears unto your eyes I'll reconcile.

Dumb show:
Enter Pericles at one door with all his train, Cleon and
Dionyza at the other. Cleon shows Pericles the tomb,
whereat Pericles makes lamentation, puts on sack-
cloth, and in a mighty passion departs. The rest go out

See how belief may suffer by foul show!
This borrowed passion stands for true old woe,
And Pericles, in sorrow all devoured,
With sighs shot through, and biggest tears o'ershowered,
Leaves Tarsus and again embarks. He swears
Never to wash his face, nor cut his hairs.
He puts on sackcloth, and to sea. He bears
A tempest which his mortal vessel tears,   30
And yet he rides it out. Now please you wit
The epitaph is for Marina writ
By wicked Dionyza.

The fairest, sweetest, and best lies here,
Who withered in her spring of year.
She was of Tyrus the King's daughter
On whom foul death hath made this slaughter.
Marina was she called, and at her birth,
Thetis being proud swallowed some part o'th'earth.
Therefore the earth, fearing to be o'erflowed,   40
Hath Thetis' birth-child on the heavens bestowed.
Wherefore she does, and swears she'll never stint,
Make raging battery upon shores of flint.

No visor does become black villainy
So well as soft and tender flattery.
Let Pericles believe his daughter's dead,

And bear his courses to be orderèd
By Lady Fortune, while our scene must play
His daughter's woe and heavy well-a-day
50 In her unholy service. Patience then,
And think you now are all in Mytilene. *Exit*

IV.5 *Enter two Gentlemen*

FIRST GENTLEMAN Did you ever hear the like?

SECOND GENTLEMAN No, nor never shall do in such a place as this, she being once gone.

FIRST GENTLEMAN But to have divinity preached there! Did you ever dream of such a thing?

SECOND GENTLEMAN No, no. Come, I am for no more bawdy houses. Shall's go hear the vestals sing?

FIRST GENTLEMAN I'll do anything now that is virtuous, but I am out of the road of rutting for ever. *Exeunt*

IV.6 *Enter the three Bawds*

PANDER Well, I had rather than twice the worth of her she had ne'er come here.

BAWD Fie, fie upon her! She's able to freeze the god Priapus and undo a whole generation. We must either get her ravished or be rid of her. When she should do for clients her fitment and do me the kindness of our profession, she has me her quirks, her reasons, her master reasons, her prayers, her knees, that she would make a puritan of the devil if he should cheapen a kiss
10 of her.

BOULT Faith, I must ravish her, or she'll disfurnish us of all our cavalleria and make our swearers priests.

PANDER Now, the pox upon her green-sickness for me!

BAWD Faith, there's no way to be rid on't but by the way

to the pox. Here comes the Lord Lysimachus disguised.

BOULT We should have both lord and lown if the peevish
baggage would but give way to customers.

Enter Lysimachus

LYSIMACHUS How now, how a dozen of virginities?

BAWD Now, the gods to bless your honour!

BOULT I am glad to see your honour in good health.   20

LYSIMACHUS You may so; 'tis the better for you that
your resorters stand upon sound legs. How now, whole-
some iniquity have you, that a man may deal withal and
defy the surgeon?

BAWD We have here one, sir, if she would – but there
never came her like in Mytilene.

LYSIMACHUS If she'd do the deeds of darkness, thou
wouldst say.

BAWD Your honour knows what 'tis to say well enough.

LYSIMACHUS Well, call forth, call forth.   30

BOULT For flesh and blood, sir, white and red, you shall
see a rose. And she were a rose indeed, if she had but –

LYSIMACHUS What, prithee?

BOULT O, sir, I can be modest.

LYSIMACHUS That dignifies the renown of a bawd no
less than it gives a good report to a number to be chaste.

Exit Boult

BAWD Here comes that which grows to the stalk, never
plucked yet, I can assure you.

Enter Boult with Marina

Is she not a fair creature?

LYSIMACHUS Faith, she would serve after a long voyage   40
at sea. Well, there's for you.

He gives her money

Leave us.

BAWD I beseech your honour, give me leave a word, and
I'll have done presently.

LYSIMACHUS I beseech you, do.

BAWD (*to Marina*) First, I would have you note this is an
honourable man.

MARINA I desire to find him so, that I may worthily note
him.

50 BAWD Next, he's the governor of this country, and a man
whom I am bound to.

MARINA If he govern the country, you are bound to him
indeed, but how honourable he is in that I know not.

BAWD Pray you, without any more virginal fencing, will
you use him kindly? He will line your apron with gold.

MARINA What he will do graciously, I will thankfully
receive.

LYSIMACHUS Ha' you done?

BAWD My lord, she's not paced yet; you must take some
60 pains to work her to your manage. Come, we will leave
his honour and her together. Go thy ways.

Exeunt Pander, Bawd, and Boult

LYSIMACHUS Now, pretty one, how long have you been
at this trade?

MARINA What trade, sir?

LYSIMACHUS Why, I cannot name it but I shall offend.

MARINA I cannot be offended with my trade. Please you
to name it.

LYSIMACHUS How long have you been of this profession?

MARINA E'er since I can remember.

70 LYSIMACHUS Did you go to't so young? Were you a
gamester at five, or at seven?

MARINA Earlier too, sir, if now I be one.

LYSIMACHUS Why, the house you dwell in proclaims you
to be a creature of sale.

MARINA Do you know this house to be a place of such
resort, and will come into't? I hear say you're of
honourable parts and are the governor of this place.

LYSIMACHUS Why, hath your principal made known
unto you who I am?

MARINA Who is my principal?   80

LYSIMACHUS Why, your herb-woman; she that sets
seeds and roots of shame and iniquity. O, you have
heard something of my power, and so stand aloof for
more serious wooing. But I protest to thee, pretty one,
my authority shall not see thee, or else look friendly
upon thee. Come, bring me to some private place.
Come, come.

MARINA
If you were born to honour, show it now;
If put upon you, make the judgement good
That thought you worthy of it.   90

LYSIMACHUS
How's this? How's this? Some more. Be sage.

MARINA   For me
That am a maid, though most ungentle fortune
Have placed me in this sty, where since I came
Diseases have been sold dearer than physic –
That the gods
Would set me free from this unhallowed place,
Though they did change me to the meanest bird
That flies i'th'purer air!

LYSIMACHUS
I did not think thou couldst have spoke so well,
Ne'er dreamt thou couldst.   100
Had I brought hither a corrupted mind,
Thy speech had altered it. Hold, here's gold for thee.
Persever in that clear way thou goest,
And the gods strengthen thee.

MARINA
The good gods preserve you.

LYSIMACHUS

    For me, be you thoughten

    That I came with no ill intent; for to me

    The very doors and windows savour vilely.

    Fare thee well. Thou art a piece of virtue, and

110   I doubt not but thy training hath been noble.

    Hold, here's more gold for thee.

    A curse upon him, die he like a thief,

    That robs thee of thy goodness! If thou

    Dost hear from me, it shall be for thy good.

       Enter Boult

BOULT I beseech your honour, one piece for me.

LYSIMACHUS

    Avaunt, thou damnèd doorkeeper!

    Your house, but for this virgin that doth prop it,

    Would sink and overwhelm you. Away!   *Exit*

BOULT How's this? We must take another course with

120   you. If your peevish chastity, which is not worth a

    breakfast in the cheapest country under the cope, shall

    undo a whole household, let me be gelded like a spaniel.

    Come your ways.

MARINA Whither would you have me?

BOULT I must have your maidenhead taken off, or the

    common hangman shall execute it. Come your ways.

    We'll have no more gentlemen driven away. Come your

    ways, I say.

       Enter Pander and Bawd

BAWD How now, what's the matter?

130 **BOULT** Worse and worse, mistress. She has here spoken

    holy words to the Lord Lysimachus.

BAWD O, abominable!

BOULT She makes our profession as it were to stink afore

    the face of the gods.

BAWD Marry, hang her up for ever!

BOULT The nobleman would have dealt with her like a
nobleman, and she sent him away as cold as a snowball,
saying his prayers too.

BAWD Boult, take her away. Use her at thy pleasure.
Crack the glass of her virginity, and make the rest 140
malleable.

BOULT An if she were a thornier piece of ground than she
is, she shall be ploughed.

MARINA Hark, hark, you gods!

BAWD She conjures! Away with her! Would she had never
come within my doors! Marry, hang you! She's born to
undo us. Will you not go the way of womenkind?
Marry come up, my dish of chastity with rosemary and
bays!   *Exeunt Pander and Bawd*

BOULT Come, mistress, come your way with me.   150

MARINA Whither wilt thou have me?

BOULT To take from you the jewel you hold so dear.

MARINA Prithee tell me one thing first.

BOULT Come now, your one thing.

MARINA What canst thou wish thine enemy to be?

BOULT Why, I could wish him to be my master, or rather
my mistress.

MARINA
  Neither of these are so bad as thou art,
  Since they do better thee in their command.
  Thou holdest a place   160
  For which the pained'st fiend of hell
  Would not in reputation change. Thou art
  The damnèd doorkeeper to every custrel
  That comes inquiring for his Tib.
  To the choleric fisting of every rogue
  Thy ear is liable. Thy food is such
  As hath been belched on by infected lungs.

BOULT What would you have me do? go to the wars,

would you? where a man may serve seven years for the
170 loss of a leg, and have not money enough in the end to
buy him a wooden one?

MARINA

Do anything but this
Thou doest. Empty old receptacles
Or common shores of filth;
Serve by indenture to the common hangman.
Any of these ways are yet better than this,
For what thou professest, a baboon, could he speak,
Would own a name too dear. That the gods
Would safely deliver me from this place!
180 Here, here's gold for thee.
If that thy master would gain by me,
Proclaim that I can sing, weave, sew, and dance,
With other virtues which I'll keep from boast,
And I will undertake all these to teach.
I doubt not but this populous city will
Yield many scholars.

BOULT But can you teach all this you speak of?

MARINA

Prove that I cannot, take me home again
And prostitute me to the basest groom
190 That doth frequent your house.

BOULT Well, I will see what I can do for thee. If I can
place thee, I will.

MARINA But amongst honest women.

BOULT Faith, my acquaintance lies little amongst them.
But since my master and mistress hath bought you,
there's no going but by their consent. Therefore I will
make them acquainted with your purpose, and I doubt
not but I shall find them tractable enough. Come, I'll
do for thee what I can. Come your ways.   *Exeunt*

✳

V CHORUS

Enter Gower

GOWER

Marina thus the brothel 'scapes, and chances
   Into an honest house, our story says.
She sings like one immortal, and she dances
   As goddess-like to her admirèd lays.
Deep clerks she dumbs, and with her neele composes
   Nature's own shape, of bud, bird, branch, or berry,
That even her art sisters the natural roses;
   Her inkle, silk, twin with the rubied cherry;
That pupils lacks she none of noble race,
   Who pour their bounty on her, and her gain   10
She gives the cursèd bawd. Here we her place,
   And to her father turn our thoughts again,
Where we left him on the sea. We there him lost,
   Where, driven before the winds, he is arrived
Here where his daughter dwells; and on this coast
   Suppose him now at anchor. The city strived
God Neptune's annual feast to keep; from whence
   Lysimachus our Tyrian ship espies,
His banners sable, trimmed with rich expense;
   And to him in his barge with fervour hies.   20
In your supposing once more put your sight;
   Of heavy Pericles, think this his bark;
Where what is done in action, more if might,
   Shall be discovered. Please you sit and hark.

Exit

Enter Helicanus. To him, two Sailors, one of Tyre and one of Mytilene

SAILOR OF TYRE (*to Sailor of Mytilene*)
Where is Lord Helicanus? He can resolve you.
O, here he is.
Sir, there is a barge put off from Mytilene,
And in it is Lysimachus, the governor,
Who craves to come aboard. What is your will?

HELICANUS
That he have his. Call up some gentlemen.

SAILOR OF TYRE Ho, gentlemen! My lord calls.
Enter two or three Gentlemen

FIRST GENTLEMAN Doth your lordship call?

HELICANUS Gentlemen, there is some of worth would
10 come aboard. I pray greet him fairly.
Exeunt Gentlemen
Enter Lysimachus and Lords, with the Gentlemen

SAILOR OF MYTILENE (*to Lysimachus*)
Sir,
This is the man that can in aught you would
Resolve you.

LYSIMACHUS Hail, reverend sir! The gods preserve you!

HELICANUS
And you, to outlive the age I am,
And die as I would do.

LYSIMACHUS   You wish me well.
Being on shore, honouring of Neptune's triumphs,
Seeing this goodly vessel ride before us,
I made to it to know of whence you are.

HELICANUS
First, what is your place?

LYSIMACHUS   I am the governor
Of this place you lie before.

20 HELICANUS   Sir,

Our vessel is of Tyre; in it the King,
A man who for this three months hath not spoken
To anyone, nor taken sustenance
But to prorogue his grief.

LYSIMACHUS
Upon what ground is his distemperature?

HELICANUS
'Twould be too tedious to repeat,
But the main grief springs from the loss
Of a belovèd daughter and a wife.

LYSIMACHUS
May we not see him?

HELICANUS   You may,
But bootless is your sight; he will not speak   30
To any.

LYSIMACHUS
Yet let me obtain my wish.

> *Helicanus draws a curtain revealing Pericles lying on*
> *a couch*

HELICANUS
Behold him. This was a goodly person,
Till the disaster that one mortal night
Drove him to this.

LYSIMACHUS
Sir King, all hail! The gods preserve you!
Hail, royal sir!

HELICANUS
It is in vain. He will not speak to you.

LORD
Sir,
We have a maid in Mytilene, I durst wager,   40
Would win some words of him.

LYSIMACHUS   'Tis well bethought.
She questionless, with her sweet harmony

123

And other chosen attractions, would allure,
And make a battery through his deafened ports,
Which now are midway stopped.
She is all happy as the fairest of all,
And with her fellow maids is now upon
The leafy shelter that abuts against
The island's side.   *Exit Lord*

HELICANUS

50 Sure, all effectless; yet nothing we'll omit
That bears recovery's name. But since your kindness
We have stretched thus far, let us beseech you
That for our gold we may provision have,
Wherein we are not destitute for want,
But weary for the staleness.

LYSIMACHUS   O, sir, a courtesy
Which if we should deny, the most just God
For every graff would send a caterpillar,
And so inflict our province. Yet once more
Let me entreat to know at large the cause
60 Of your king's sorrow.

HELICANUS

Sit, sir. I will recount it to you. But see,
I am prevented.
        Enter Lord, with Marina and her companion

LYSIMACHUS

O, here's the lady that I sent for.
Welcome, fair one! Is't not a goodly presence?

HELICANUS

She's a gallant lady.

LYSIMACHUS

She's such a one that, were I well assured
Came of a gentle kind and noble stock,
I'd wish no better choice, and think me rarely wed.
Fair one, all goodness that consists in beauty,

Expect even here, where is a kingly patient,   70
If that thy prosperous and artificial feat
Can draw him but to answer thee in aught,
Thy sacred physic shall receive such pay
As thy desires can wish.

MARINA   Sir, I will use
My utmost skill in his recovery, provided
That none but I and my companion maid
Be suffered to come near him.

LYSIMACHUS   Come, let us leave her,
And the gods make her prosperous.

They withdraw
Marina sings

LYSIMACHUS (*coming forward*)
Marked he your music?

MARINA   No, nor looked on us.

LYSIMACHUS (*withdrawing*)
See, she will speak to him.   80

MARINA
Hail, sir! My lord, lend ear.

PERICLES
Hum, ha!

He pushes her away

MARINA
I am a maid,
My lord, that ne'er before invited eyes,
But have been gazed on like a comet. She speaks,
My lord, that maybe hath endured a grief
Might equal yours, if both were justly weighed.
Though wayward fortune did malign my state,
My derivation was from ancestors
Who stood equivalent with mighty kings.   90
But time hath rooted out my parentage,
And to the world and awkward casualties

125

Bound me in servitude. (*Aside*) I will desist,
But there is something glows upon my cheek,
And whispers in mine ear 'Go not till he speak.'

PERICLES

My fortunes – parentage – good parentage –
To equal mine – was it not thus? What say you?

MARINA

I said, my lord, if you did know my parentage,
You would not do me violence.

PERICLES

100 I do think so. Pray you, turn your eyes upon me.
You're like something that – What countrywoman?
Here of these shores?

MARINA   No, nor of any shores,
Yet I was mortally brought forth, and am
No other than I appear.

PERICLES

I am great with woe, and shall deliver weeping.
My dearest wife was like this maid,
And such a one my daughter might have been.
My queen's square brows, her stature to an inch,
As wand-like straight, as silver-voiced,
110 Her eyes as jewel-like, and cased as richly,
In pace another Juno;
Who starves the ears she feeds, and makes them hungry
The more she gives them speech. Where do you live?

MARINA

Where I am but a stranger. From the deck
You may discern the place.

PERICLES   Where were you bred?
And how achieved you these endowments which
You make more rich to owe?

MARINA

If I should tell my history, it would seem

Like lies disdained in the reporting.

PERICLES   Prithee speak.
Falseness cannot come from thee, for thou lookest   120
Modest as justice, and thou seemest a palace
For the crowned truth to dwell in. I will believe thee,
And make my senses credit thy relation
To points that seem impossible, for thou lookest
Like one I loved indeed. What were thy friends?
Didst thou not say, when I did push thee back –
Which was when I perceived thee – that thou camest
From good descending?

MARINA   So indeed I did.

PERICLES
Report thy parentage. I think thou saidst
Thou hadst been tossed from wrong to injury,   130
And that thou thought'st thy griefs might equal mine,
If both were opened.

MARINA   Some such thing I said,
And said no more but what my thoughts
Did warrant me was likely.

PERICLES   Tell thy story.
If thine considered prove the thousandth part
Of my endurance, thou art a man, and I
Have suffered like a girl; yet thou dost look
Like Patience gazing on kings' graves and smiling
Extremity out of act. What were thy friends?
How lost thou them? Thy name, my most kind virgin? 140
Recount, I do beseech thee. Come, sit by me.

MARINA
My name is Marina.

PERICLES   O, I am mocked,
And thou by some incensèd god sent hither
To make the world to laugh at me.

MARINA   Patience, good sir,

Or here I'll cease.

PERICLES   Nay, I'll be patient.
Thou little knowest how thou dost startle me
To call thyself Marina.

MARINA   The name
Was given me by one that had some power,
My father, and a king.

PERICLES   How, a king's daughter?
And called Marina?

150 MARINA   You said you would believe me,
But, not to be a troubler of your peace,
I will end here.

PERICLES   But are you flesh and blood?
Have you a working pulse? And are no fairy?
Motion as well? Speak on. Where were you born?
And wherefore called Marina?

MARINA   Called Marina
For I was born at sea.

PERICLES   At sea! what mother?

MARINA

My mother was the daughter of a king;
Who died the minute I was born,
As my good nurse Lychorida hath oft
Delivered weeping.

160 PERICLES   O, stop there a little!
This is the rarest dream
That e'er dull sleep did mock sad fools withal.
This cannot be my daughter, buried!
Well, where were you bred?
I'll hear you more, to the bottom of your story,
And never interrupt you.

MARINA   You scorn to believe me,
'Twere best I did give o'er.

PERICLES   I will believe you

By the syllable of what you shall deliver.
Yet give me leave: how came you in these parts?
Where were you bred? 170

MARINA

The King my father did in Tarsus leave me,
Till cruel Cleon with his wicked wife
Did seek to murder me;
And having wooed a villain to attempt it,
Who having drawn to do't,
A crew of pirates came and rescued me,
Brought me to Mytilene. But, good sir,
Whither will you have me? Why do you weep? It may
     be
You think me an impostor. No, good faith!
I am the daughter to King Pericles, 180
If good King Pericles be.

PERICLES   Ho, Helicanus!

HELICANUS

Calls my lord?

PERICLES

Thou art a grave and noble counsellor,
Most wise in general. Tell me, if thou canst,
What this maid is, or what is like to be,
That thus hath made me weep.

HELICANUS   I know not,
But here's the regent, sir, of Mytilene
Speaks nobly of her.

LYSIMACHUS   She never would tell
Her parentage. Being demanded that,
She would sit still and weep. 190

PERICLES

O Helicanus, strike me, honoured sir,
Give me a gash, put me to present pain,
Lest this great sea of joys rushing upon me

O'erbear the shores of my mortality
And drown me with their sweetness. O, come hither,
Thou that beget'st him that did thee beget;
Thou that wast born at sea, buried at Tarsus,
And found at sea again. O Helicanus,
Down on thy knees; thank the holy gods as loud
200 As thunder threatens us. This is Marina.
What was thy mother's name? Tell me but that,
For truth can never be confirmed enough,
Though doubts did ever sleep.

MARINA   First, sir, I pray,
What is your title?

PERICLES
I am Pericles of Tyre; but tell me now
My drowned queen's name, as in the rest you said
Thou hast been god-like perfect, and thou art
The heir of kingdoms, and another life
To Pericles thy father.

MARINA
210 Is it no more to be your daughter than
To say my mother's name was Thaisa?
Thaisa was my mother, who did end
The minute I began.

PERICLES
Now blessing on thee! Rise; thou art my child.
Give me fresh garments. Mine own, Helicanus!
She is not dead at Tarsus, as she should have been,
By savage Cleon. She shall tell thee all;
When thou shalt kneel, and justify in knowledge
She is thy very princess. Who is this?

HELICANUS
220 Sir, 'tis the governor of Mytilene
Who, hearing of your melancholy state,
Did come to see you.

PERICLES   I embrace you.
  Give me my robes. I am wild in my beholding.
  O, heavens bless my girl! But hark, what music?
  Tell Helicanus, my Marina, tell him
  O'er, point by point, for yet he seems to doubt,
  How sure you are my daughter. But what music?
HELICANUS
  My lord, I hear none.
PERICLES   None?
  The music of the spheres! List, my Marina!
LYSIMACHUS
  It is not good to cross him; give him way.   230
PERICLES
  Rarest sounds! Do ye not hear?
LYSIMACHUS   Music, my lord?
PERICLES
  I hear most heavenly music.
  It nips me unto listening, and thick slumber
  Hangs upon mine eyes. Let me rest.
    He sleeps
LYSIMACHUS
  A pillow for his head. So, leave him all.
  Well, my companion friends,
  If this but answer to my just belief,
  I'll well remember you.   *Exeunt all but Pericles*
    Diana appears to Pericles in a vision
DIANA
  My temple stands in Ephesus. Hie thee thither,
  And do upon mine altar sacrifice.   240
  There, when my maiden priests are met together,
  Before the people all,
  Reveal how thou at sea didst lose thy wife.
  To mourn thy crosses, with thy daughter's call,
  And give them repetition to the life.

Or perform my bidding, or thou livest in woe;
Do't, and happy, by my silver bow.
Awake, and tell thy dream.   *Exit*

PERICLES (*waking*)
Celestial Dian, goddess argentine,
I will obey thee. Helicanus!
    Enter Helicanus, Lysimachus, and Marina

250 HELICANUS   Sir?

PERICLES
My purpose was for Tarsus, there to strike
The inhospitable Cleon, but I am
For other service first. Toward Ephesus
Turn our blown sails. Eftsoons I'll tell thee why.
(*To Lysimachus*)
Shall we refresh us, sir, upon your shore,
And give you gold for such provision
As our intents will need?

LYSIMACHUS   Sir,
With all my heart; and when you come ashore,
I have another suit.

PERICLES   You shall prevail,
260 Were it to woo my daughter, for it seems
You have been noble towards her.

LYSIMACHUS
Sir, lend me your arm.

PERICLES   Come, my Marina.   *Exeunt*

V.2   *Enter Gower*

GOWER
Now our sands are almost run;
More a little, and then dumb.
This my last boon give me,
For such kindness must relieve me,

That you aptly will suppose
What pageantry, what feats, what shows,
What minstrelsy, and pretty din
The regent made in Mytilene
To greet the King. So he thrived
That he is promised to be wived   10
To fair Marina, but in no wise
Till he had done his sacrifice
As Dian bade; whereto being bound,
The interim, pray you, all confound.
In feathered briefness sails are filled,
And wishes fall out as they're willed.
At Ephesus the temple see,
Our king, and all his company.
That he can hither come so soon
Is by your fancies' thankful doom.   *Exit* 20

Enter on one side Thaisa and virgin priestesses of **V.3**
Diana, Cerimon, and other inhabitants of Ephesus;
on the other side, Pericles, Marina, Lysimachus,
Helicanus, and Lords

PERICLES

Hail, Dian! To perform thy just command
I here confess myself the King of Tyre,
Who, frighted from my country, did wed
At Pentapolis the fair Thaisa.
At sea in childbed died she, but brought forth
A maid-child called Marina, who, O goddess,
Wears yet thy silver livery. She at Tarsus
Was nursed with Cleon, whom at fourteen years
He sought to murder. But her better stars
Brought her to Mytilene; 'gainst whose shore   10
Riding, her fortunes brought the maid aboard us,

Where, by her own most clear remembrance, she
Made known herself my daughter.

THAISA   Voice and favour!
You are, you are – O royal Pericles!
   She faints

PERICLES
What means the nun? She dies! Help, gentlemen!

CERIMON
Noble sir,
If you have told Diana's altar true,
This is your wife.

PERICLES   Reverend appearer, no;
I threw her overboard with these very arms.

CERIMON
Upon this coast, I warrant you.

20 PERICLES   'Tis most certain.

CERIMON
Look to the lady. O, she's but overjoyed.
Early one blustering morn this lady was
Thrown upon this shore. I oped the coffin,
Found there rich jewels, recovered her, and placed her
Here in Diana's temple.

PERICLES   May we see them?

CERIMON
Great sir, they shall be brought you to my house,
Whither I invite you. Look,
Thaisa is recovered.

THAISA   O, let me look.
If he be none of mine, my sanctity
30 Will to my sense bend no licentious ear,
But curb it, spite of seeing. O, my lord,
Are you not Pericles? Like him you spake,
Like him you are. Did you not name a tempest,
A birth, and death?

PERICLES   The voice of dead Thaisa!

THAISA

 That Thaisa am I,
 Supposèd dead and drowned.

PERICLES

 Immortal Dian!

THAISA   Now I know you better:
 When we with tears parted Pentapolis,
 The King my father gave you such a ring.

PERICLES

 This, this! No more, you gods; your present kindness 40
 Makes my past miseries sports; you shall do well
 That on the touching of her lips I may
 Melt, and no more be seen. O, come, be buried
 A second time within these arms.

MARINA   My heart
 Leaps to be gone into my mother's bosom.
  She kneels

PERICLES

 Look who kneels here; flesh of thy flesh, Thaisa,
 Thy burden at the sea, and called Marina
 For she was yielded there.

THAISA   Blest, and mine own!

HELICANUS Hail, madam, and my queen!

THAISA   I know you not.

PERICLES

 You have heard me say, when I did fly from Tyre, 50
 I left behind an ancient substitute.
 Can you remember what I called the man?
 I have named him oft.

THAISA   'Twas Helicanus then.

PERICLES

 Still confirmation.
 Embrace him, dear Thaisa, this is he.

Now do I long to hear how you were found,
How possibly preserved, and who to thank,
Besides the gods, for this great miracle.

THAISA

Lord Cerimon, my lord; this man
60 Through whom the gods have shown their power; that can
From first to last resolve you.

PERICLES   Reverend sir,
The gods can have no mortal officer
More like a god than you. Will you deliver
How this dead queen re-lives?

CERIMON   I will, my lord.
Beseech you first, go with me to my house,
Where shall be shown you all was found with her,
How she came placed here in the temple;
No needful thing omitted.

PERICLES   Pure Dian,
I bless thee for thy vision, and
70 Will offer night-oblations to thee. Thaisa,
This prince, the fair betrothèd of your daughter,
Shall marry her at Pentapolis. And now,
This ornament,
Makes me look dismal, will I clip to form,
And what this fourteen years no razor touched,
To grace thy marriage-day, I'll beautify.

THAISA

Lord Cerimon hath letters of good credit, sir,
My father's dead.

PERICLES

Heavens make a star of him! Yet there, my queen,
80 We'll celebrate their nuptials, and ourselves
Will in that kingdom spend our following days.
Our son and daughter shall in Tyrus reign.

Lord Cerimon, we do our longing stay
To hear the rest untold. Sir, lead's the way.   *Exeunt*

EPILOGUE

Enter Gower

GOWER
In Antiochus and his daughter you have heard
Of monstrous lust the due and just reward;
In Pericles, his queen, and daughter seen,
Although assailed with fortune fierce and keen,
Virtue preserved from fell destruction's blast,
Led on by heaven, and crowned with joy at last.
In Helicanus may you well descry
A figure of truth, of faith, of loyalty.
In reverend Cerimon there well appears
The worth that learnèd charity aye wears.   10
For wicked Cleon and his wife, when fame
Had spread his cursèd deed to the honoured name
Of Pericles, to rage the city turn,
That him and his they in his palace burn.
The gods for murder seemèd to consent
To punish, although not done, but meant.
So on your patience evermore attending,
New joy wait on you! Here our play has ending.
                                              Exit

COMMENTARY

'Q' refers to the first edition of the play, published in quarto form in 1609. 'Wilkins' refers to *The Painful Adventures of Pericles, Prince of Tyre* by George Wilkins, published in 1608; quotations (modernized) and page numbers are from the text in Volume VI (1966) of *Narrative and Dramatic Sources of Shakespeare*, edited by Geoffrey Bullough.

The Characters in the Play

The episodic nature of *Pericles* makes it easy to double many of the parts in this large cast. Obvious doublings are the three Fishermen of Pentapolis with the Bawd, Pander, and Boult of the Mytilene brothel. Antiochus probably doubled with Simonides (and possibly Lysimachus), his daughter with Thaisa or Marina. There are many possible combinations. It has become a fashion on the English stage to double Marina and Thaisa. This unfortunate experiment contradicts the play's insistence that the daughter does *not* take the mother's place. See the Introduction, page 27. Both in this play and in *The Winter's Tale* (in which the doubling of Hermione and Perdita has been tried out on the stage) Shakespeare tried to prevent doubling by bringing both mother and daughter on stage together in the last scene.

I *Chorus*

2   *ancient Gower.* John Gower (?1330–1408) had told the story of Pericles in his *Confessio Amantis*, and his version is the main source for the play. He wrote in the same metre as this chorus.

6   *ember-eves.* Ember days were four periods of fasting

and prayer, one for each season of the year; *ember-eve* was the preceding vigil.

6   *holidays* (probably a weakening of the original text, which would have rhymed. 'Whitsun-ales' has been suggested. 'Holy-ales' is often printed, but the expression is not known to exist.)

8   *for restoratives* for its healing power

9   *purchase* beneficial result

10   *Et bonum quo antiquius eo melius* and the older a good thing is, the better

12   *wit's more ripe* wisdom is superior

13   *that* if

14   *to your wishes* as you would wish

16   *taper-light* candle-light

17   *This Antioch, then* this is Antioch, then. Antioch (actually founded about 300 B.C.) was the capital of Syria, on the river Orontes.

        Antiochus the Great (223–187 B.C. He ruled the Asian empire inherited by his forefathers from Alexander the Great. He eventually clashed with the Romans and was defeated by them.)

20   *authors* authorities. The line has a reasonably authentic medieval touch.

21   *peer* mate. Most editions read 'fere' (companion).

23   *buxom* lively, cheerful. Compare Milton's *L'Allegro*, line 24: 'So buxom, blithe, and debonair'.

24   *As* as if

25   *liking* a lustful affection

29   *custom* by custom

32   *frame* direct their course

38   *His riddle told not* if he couldn't explain Antiochus's riddle

39   *wight* person

40   *yon grim looks* (the heads of the executed princes. This is an interesting hint at the 'scenery' provided for the play. Wilkins refers to them as 'placed upon his castle wall' (page 498); probably the balustrade of the

gallery or 'lords' room' at the back of the stage was used.)

41–2   *What now ensues . . . best can justify.* The repetition of the previous couplet's rhyme and the sudden change to a ten-syllable line argue that this couplet is corrupt. It is probably a garbled conflation of two couplets. The audience is now to judge Gower's tale not from what he says but from what they see; and he submits his material, or case (*cause*), to those best able to make it appear true (*justify*), namely, the actors. The last line has to be filled out: 'I give my cause to those who can best justify it.'

I.1   (stage direction) *Prince Pericles*. In all previous versions of the widely-told story, the hero had been called Apollonius. The change to 'Pericles' has led commentators to ask whether the dramatist had in mind the great Greek statesman, or perhaps Pyrocles, the hero of Sidney's *Arcadia*, which is drawn on in the play. The simple truth may be that the dramatist liked the sound of the name and it fitted a blank-verse line better than Apollonius.

1   *Tyre* (an ancient Phoenician trading city on an island off the coast of Syria; now Sur in the Lebanon)
  at large received fully comprehended

9   *Lucina* (the name for Juno or Diana in her attribute as goddess presiding over childbirth; compare III.1.10)

10   *dowry*. It is uncertain whether this refers to the girl's beauty or to the calling together of the planets.
  to glad her presence to make her presence a gladness to the world. This use of words is very clumsy.

11–12   *The senate-house of planets . . . perfections.* She was given the best astrological send-off that could be arranged (the position of the planets at the moment of birth being of vital importance). The image is borrowed from Sidney's *Arcadia*, 'The senate-house of the planets . . . set for the decreeing of perfection in man'.

14   *Graces her subjects* with Graces for her subjects

17   *curious* exquisite

19   *her mild companion* (nonsensical; the intended meaning is 'companion of one so mild')

28   *Hesperides* (properly the daughters of Hesperus, in whose garden grew the golden apples, guarded by a dragon; but the Elizabethans often used the word to mean the garden itself. One of the labours of Hercules was to obtain the apples. By way of rejoinder, Antiochus here gives a grim extension to the image used by Pericles at line 22 above, though the force of his repartee is blunted in the text as we have it.)

29   *dangerous to be touched*. The repetition of *touch* and *dangerous* with reference to the daughter at lines 88–90 below suggests that one passage has influenced the other in the reporter's mind.

30   *deathlike* (a deliberate archaism) deadly

32   *countless glory*. This very awkward phrase has probably come into being because of a muddling in the reporter's mind of this speech with a later one in which we also find the words *heaven*, *countless*, *view* (see line 74).
desert must gain. The idea that the power to solve a riddle is a measure of a man's excellence is very ancient, as the story of Oedipus and the Sphinx shows. Nearer home, it is the basis for the choosing of the caskets in *The Merchant of Venice*.

33–4   *And which without desert because thine eye|Presumes to reach*. There is a muddle here; the meaning aimed at seems to be 'but if your eye presumes to aspire without desert . . .'.

34   *all the whole heap must die*. There is an antithesis between the offence of the part (*eye*) and the punishment of the entire man, but the use of *the whole heap* to refer to the body of a human being is so absurd that we assume there is corruption here.

35   *Yon . . . princes.* See I Chorus 40 and note.

36   *adventurous* imprudently bold. The spelling of Q,
        'aduentrous', indicates the three-syllable pronuncia-
        tion.

37   *semblance* appearance

41   *For* from

46   *death remembered should be like a mirror* to concentrate
        the mind on the image of death (the skull or death's-
        head) is to realize that it is one's own image one is
        looking at. This telescoped image, appearing within
        such a jog-trot couplet, strengthens one's feeling that
        there is poetry underneath rather than *in* these lines;
        see the Introduction, pages 37–40.

49   *Who know the world, see heaven, but feeling woe.* This is
        probably a compression of the original. The general
        sense is that at the approach of death men see heaven,
        and by comparison the world becomes despicable to
        them; in spite of pain, they have no wish for health
        and a continuance of life.

50   *Gripe* clutch
        erst formerly

57   *conclusion* riddle. This is a very rare usage, but it is
        found in Gower's *Confessio Amantis*, and it seems to be
        another deliberate archaism.

60   *all 'sayed yet* all who have so far assayed (attempted)
        the task; or, all who have so far been assayed (put to
        the trial). Q reads 'sayd' for 'sayed.

62   *assume* undertake, enter upon
        lists combat

63–4   *Nor ask advice . . . faithfulness and courage* (another
        borrowing from the *Arcadia*: 'asking no advice of
        no thought, but of faithfulness and courage').
        This is presumably Pericles' rejoinder to Antiochus's
        Scorning advice six lines before; it seems a little
        misplaced.

64   (stage direction) *He reads aloud.* Wilkins's words give
        us some idea of the staging here: 'the tyrant . . . with

an angry brow, threw down the riddle ... which the Prince taking up read aloud' (page 498).

65 *viper.* The viper's young were supposed to eat their way out of their mother's womb.

68 *father* (to be pronounced 'feyther' to give a near-rhyme to *labour*)

69–70 *He's father, son ... his child.* This confusion of relationships is contrasted with the paradox of the spiritual relationship of Pericles and Marina at the end of the play. See the note to V.1.196, and the Introduction, pages 27–8.

71 *they.* Wilkins gives this riddle almost word for word but here reads 'this', which may be the correct reading.

74 *gives.* This use of the singular form for the plural is quite often found, and should not be regarded as an error.

  countless eyes (the stars)

77 *Fair glass of light.* The image is perhaps of a beautiful glass vessel which contains poison, but the transition to *casket* in the next line is abrupt; the text may be corrupt.

80 *on whom perfections wait.* The phrase has little meaning and one suspects that the need for a rhyme is responsible for it.

82 *viol.* The treble viol and the bass viol were the forerunners of the violin and the cello.

  sense senses (but the image is not clear)

88 *touch not.* As Pericles is making his elaborate comparison between sexual relations and playing the viol, he may (though still speaking 'aside') move towards the daughter with his hand outstretched.

90 *dangerous.* See the note to line 29.

94 *braid* upbraid

97–101 *vice repeated ... hurt them.* It seems that a powerful simile has been compressed and confused in these lines. The meaning of the original may have been as follows: 'To talk about the vice of powerful people is to behave like the wind, which, in spreading itself, only raises a dust which hurts people. The one who talks about the vice is soon got rid of, and those who have listened to him have learned no more than not to listen another time.' Many commentators make *the sore eyes* those of the sinful monarch, but they must be the same as the *others' eyes* of line 98.

101–3 *The blind mole . . . die for't.* This celebrated image, often hailed as Shakespearian, stands out in the lame verse of this scene and may indicate the quality of much that has been lost. Even so, it is not free from suspicion of corruption. The *poor worm* is generally taken to mean the mole; it was common to use 'worm' as a pitying endearment. But it is an odd coincidence that molehills are a sign of the death of worms, who are the chief food of moles. If the worm is the mole, the passage means that if you proclaim tyranny you will suffer for it. If the worm is the earthworm, the more subtle point implied in the previous passage is continued: to proclaim tyranny is to make other people, innocent non-partisans, suffer. There is a case for supposing that these lines originally conveyed an application of the obvious fact in nature that molehills (which lead to the finding and killing of moles) cause the death of both the mole and the worm.

102 *Copped* humped
thronged crushed

108 *All love the womb that their first being bred.* This puts the incest the wrong way round, son and mother. The feeble couplets which surround this line are characteristic of the rewriting which it is suggested the reporter is responsible for (see the Introduction, pages 35–8), and it may well be that the original alluded to the mother/daughter issue which is so important in the play. Antiochus takes as partner the fruit of the womb of his proper partner.

111 *gloze* speak fair words

114   *cancel of* cancellation of, extinction of. Q reads 'counsell of'.

115–16   *Yet hope ... otherwise.* These two lines again suggest unintelligent compression. The original may have spoken of the hope of fruitful deeds *from so fair a tree.*

118   *our secret* (the riddle)

120   *entertain* entertainment

129   *untimely.* In the corresponding passage in Wilkins (page 500) the word is 'uncomely'. Some editors adopt this, but it seems feeble in the context, while *untimely* suggests the grossness of the mingling of the generations.

136   *Blush not* who blush not

141   *targets* shields
        put off keep away

142   *cropped* cut off, reaped
        clear free from accusation

144   A new scene should begin here on the clearance of the stage as Pericles goes out. Wilkins supports this: 'Antiochus being now private in his lodging ...' (page 500). The early editors continued the scene, however, and it is now too late to alter the traditional divisions.

144–60   The verse now becomes very irregular. It is possible to redivide short passages to provide rather more convincing verse, but as a whole this section is neither regular verse nor prose.

153   *partakes* communicates

165   *level* take aim

167–8   *pistol's length* range of pistol shot (an anachronism)

168   *sure* harmless

I.2   The action of this scene at Tyre has been badly muddled and abbreviated; it is one of the most corrupt in the play. With the help of Wilkins (pages 500–501), it is not difficult to see how it ought to go. Pericles entered with his lords, who greeted him on his return. (The corrupt and misplaced version of this may be at lines 34–6.) He dismissed them curtly, asking them to watch the harbour for approaching ships (compare lines 48–50). After the soliloquy, Helicanus entered and was bold enough to take the prince to task for his bad humour. (The text misses this altogether.) Helicanus defended his temerity on the grounds that straight-speaking is better than flattery. Pericles was at first angry, but then forgave him and told him his troubles. The person reconstructing the play lacked essential pieces and strove rather helplessly to create some kind of continuity.

3   *used* customary

4   *the day's glorious walk* the progress of the sun

9   *joy* make joyful

12   *misdread* (an intensification of 'dread', but the *O.E.D.* has no other example of the noun)

13   *care* anxiety, worry

15   *cares it be not done* is anxious that it should not be done

20   *boots it me* is it any good to me

     honour. To complete the metre, 'him' is usually added, but it makes an awkward chime with the next line.

25   *the ostent* the display. Q reads 'the stint', which could be either a mishearing or a misreading. The original may have been 'th' ostent'.

33   *punish that before that he would punish* punish in advance him whom Antiochus wishes to punish

34–7 See the headnote to this scene. The greetings of the lords must be wrong; it is absurd for the Second Lord to bid adieu at this point. And their harmless words are no cue for a tirade against flattery.

41   *wind.* Q reads 'sparke', which is almost certainly the compositor's repetition of the word from the previous line. Editors usually read 'blast', which seems strong for a bellows.

44   *Signor Sooth* Sir Sweet Talk

48   *cares* watchfulness
        o'erlook scrutinize

49   *lading* cargo

51   *moved* angered

58   *Do but you strike* it remains only for you to strike

61   *let their ears hear their faults hid* allow themselves to listen to speeches which conceal their faults

72   *purchase* acquisition, prize

74   *Are arms* which are arms. *Issue* is taken as plural, but the phrase is so clumsy one suspects its genuineness.

78   *smooth* to flatter, conciliate

81   *careful* watchful

86   *he doubt* he suspect

89   *unlaid ope* unrevealed

90   *lop that doubt* get rid of that fear

92   *mine – if I may call – offence* my offence – if I am to call it that

93   *who* which

95   *now reprovedst* didst just now reprove

108   *the destinies* (goddesses of destiny; the Fates)

109   *Your rule direct* hand over your responsibilities as ruler

112   *my liberties.* This can mean either 'my domains' or 'the rights of my subjects'.

115   *Tarsus* (a city on the river Cydnus in Cilicia; here and elsewhere spelt 'Tharsus' in Q)

122   The awkward sense and defective rhyme-scheme have led to the conjecture that a line had dropped out between 121 and 122.

123   *time of both this truth shall ne'er convince* time shall never disprove this truth about the two of us

124   *shine* shining light

I.3.4–6   *a wise fellow ... his secrets.* Plutarch tells of the poet Philippides who, when the ruler Lysimachus asked what he might give him, said 'Even what it shall please thee, O King, so it be none of thy secrets' (*Life of Demetrius*).

8   *indenture* contract of service
         Husht! Compare the more common 'whisht!'.

13   *gone to travel* set off on a journey. An unusual example
         of 'go to', meaning 'set about' or 'proceed to' some-
         thing, which is more familiar in such phrases as 'go to
         work', 'go to war'.

16   *unlicensed of your loves* without the assent you would
         lovingly have given

21   *doubting* fearing

22   *he'd correct himself* he wished to punish himself

25–9   The whole of this scene is printed as prose in Q,
         although some of the speeches are clearly verse. Some
         editors divide Thaliard's speech into awkward verse,
         but although the original may have been verse it is
         hardly so now.

26–7   *the King's seas must please.* Something has gone wrong
         here. One ingenious emendation is 'the King's ears it
         must please'. The corrupt phrase may hide one of two
         meanings: (1) the King will have to be satisfied with
         the news; (2) the seas will have to do the King's
         bidding (and kill Pericles).

36–7   *We have no reason ... not to us.* This is the now
         familiar telescoped form of rewriting. The intended
         meaning was either 'We have no reason to desire your
         immediate departure, even though your message was
         directed to our master, not to us' or 'We have no
         reason to wish to accept the message, since it was
         directed to our master, not to us'.

I.4.5   *digs* excavates

8–9   *Here they are but felt ... higher rise.* This woeful
         couplet is best not searched for meaning. The general
         idea is probably 'Things are bad enough if we accept
         them as they are; if we seek to make things better, we
         may make things worse.'

9   *topped* pruned, lopped

13   *force us* (an editorial addition which tries to bring a glimmer of meaning to a passage which is nonsense in Q)

17   *helpers*. Many editors read 'helps'. It may seem wrong that, if heaven slumbers, the sad cries should awaken heaven's helpers, but it is possible that the word *helpers* is correct, and the rest of the sentence corrupt. The original may have had the idea of the cries waking heaven and making them send their helpers (such as Pericles is).

21   *This Tarsus*. The sentence is never completed.

22   *on whom plenty held full hand* over whom plenty poured her gifts with unrestrained hand. The image is of the cornucopia.

23   *herself*. *Riches* is considered as a feminine singular noun, 'wealth'.

26   *jetted* strutted
      adorned adorned themselves

27   *Like one another's glass to trim them by* as though they were acting as one another's mirror to help them dress

31   *The name of help grew odious to repeat*. This line is ridiculously wrong. In these circumstances of proud luxury, the whole idea of needing assistance would be irrelevant.

37   *defiled* made filthy. Presumably the idea of decay was more prominent in the original.

39   *not yet two summers younger*. The reading of *summers* for Q's 'sauers' is confirmed by Wilkins, who gives the phrase a more likely context: 'to see the power of change, that this their city, who, not two summers younger, did so excel in pomp' (page 502).

40   *inventions* specially devised novelties

42   *nuzzle up* rear, bring up (with suggestions of nourishing and nestling)

43   *curious* choice, carefully prepared

46   *to lengthen life* in order to lengthen the life of the other

47   *Here stands a lord and there a lady weeping*. Wilkins

has a more convincing version: 'here stands one weeping, and there lies another dying' (page 503).

54   *superfluous riots* extravagant dissipation or revelry
        these tears this lamentation

61   *portly sail* stately fleet
        make hitherward shaping their course in our direction

70   *Whereas no glory's got to overcome* in which conquest there is no glory to be obtained

71   *That's the least fear* that's not in the least to be feared

74   *like him's untutored to repeat* like one who hasn't been taught to recite (the maxim which follows)

78   *Our ground's the lowest and we are half-way there* (a clumsy version of the common saying that he who is lying on the ground has no further to fall)

83   *on peace consist* is determined on peace

91   *But to relieve them of their heavy load.* Presumably in the original it was people rather than tears who were to be relieved of their burden.

92   *you happily may think* which you may perhaps think

93   *was* which was

94   *bloody veins expecting overthrow* (perhaps a compression of an original image which suggested that the blood-vessels of the Trojan horse brought a bloody overthrow to Troy)

101–4   Cleon's speech looks forward to the criminal ingratitude of Dionyza at the beginning of Act IV.

101   *gratify* show gratitude or affection towards

104   *succeed* follow

II *Chorus*

2   *iwis* assuredly

4   *awful* worthy of respect and deference

9   *conversation* conduct, manners

10   *benison* blessing

12   *Thinks all is writ he speken can* thinks everything he

speaks is gospel. *Speken* is a medievalism, like *been* (line 28), *perishen* (line 35), *escapend* (line 36).

13   *remember* commemorate

15   *to the contrary.* The tidings are contrary in the sense that they are bad tidings; but the line may be corrupt.

18   *Not to eat honey.* The sense requires 'did not intend to eat honey'. This passage is corrupt, but allowances must be made for the reporter's attempts to reproduce the author's attempts to reproduce medieval English.

19   *forthy* therefore. Q reads 'for though', which is impossible. Gower frequently uses 'forthi' and 'forthy' in *Confessio Amantis*.

24   *hid intent . . . murder.* Q's original reading was 'hid in Tent . . . murdred', but after some copies had been printed this was changed to 'had intent . . . murder'. Printers of this period habitually made proof corrections during the printing run, often without checking the manuscript; in this case it seems likely that the change from 'hid in Tent' to 'had intent' was a guess, clever but wrong.

27   *doing so* doing as advised

32   *Should* which should

35   *pelf* possessions

36   *Ne aught escapend* and no one escaping

40   *longs* belongs to

II.1.6   *left my breath.* The sentence is probably corrupt, but the usual alteration to 'left me breath' is unhelpful. *Breath* here has the sense of 'life', and the general meaning is that there is nothing left for him in life but the contemplation of death.

12   *Pilch* (literally a leather coat or jerkin)

17   *with a wanion* with a vengeance

22   *well-a-day* alas

24   *the porpoise* (commonly regarded as a forerunner of stormy weather)

26–9   *I marvel how the fishes live in the sea? . . . the great ones eat up the little ones.* This was a common saying. There is a close relation between the version here and one in John Day's *Law Tricks*, also printed in 1608, though it may be an earlier play than *Pericles*.

28   *a-land* on land (the same formation as 'ashore', 'afloat')

30   *'a* he

30–31   *plays and tumbles.* Compare *bounced and tumbled* in line 24. Echoes of this kind are marks of reported texts.

33   *a-th'land* on the land

48   *the finny subject of the sea.* Q reads 'fenny' for *finny*. Wilkins has 'the finny subjects of the sea' (page 506). *Subject* is a legitimate use of the singular to indicate a class (for example, 'the farmer', 'the housewife').

50   *recollect* gather up

51   *may men approve or men detect* may commend men or reveal their guilt

54–5   *If it be . . . look after it.* No one has been able to explain this passage. Perhaps a line has fallen out. 'Scratch it out' has been proposed instead of *search out*. *Fits you* is probably the colloquial 'get the better of you', as in the common phrase 'I'll fit you'. Perhaps the underlying idea is that this must be the castaway's unlucky day and it ought to be struck out of the calendar. But the play on *Honest* remains a problem.

58   *cast.* The Fisherman uses the word with its common secondary sense of 'vomit'.

60   *In that vast tennis-court . . . the ball.* It was a common saying that men were like tennis-balls to the gods or to Fortune. Wilkins talks of Pericles as the tennis-ball to Fortune, but Q is more likely to be right here, since the notion of the sea as a vast tennis-court where the waters and the wind play with man relates this passage to the storm scene in III.1, where Pericles appeals to *The god of this great vast* (Neptune) and to the god of the winds (Aeolus).

67   *practised* engaged in (professionally)

73   *thronged up with* crushed, overwhelmed by

74-7   The thin and flat writing of the latter half of Pericles'
        speech is in strong contrast to the vigour of the prose
        given to the Fishermen. It is probable that the prose is
        much more authentic than the verse. See the Intro-
        duction, page 37.

78   *quotha* indeed (literally, 'quoth he'; Q prints 'ke-tha')
        an if (with the sense of 'so long as'). The rough
        humour of the idea of helping the gods in this practical
        way is typical of the Fishermen.

80   *afore me* upon my word

81   *flesh* butcher's meat

82   *puddings* large sausages

85-6   *you said you could not beg?* (ironical wonderment at the
        success of Pericles' appeal)

100   *Pentapolis* (the five cities of Cyrenaica on the North
        African coast including the modern Benghazi, in what
        is now Libya)

110   *tourney* take part in a tournament

114   *things must be as they may.* It was proverbial that 'he
        that cannot do as he would must do as he may'.

115-16 *what a man ... wife's soul.* This is another garbled
        joke, the meaning of which has gone beyond recall.
        It has been suggested that we should read 'steal' for
        deal, but there is too much else that is unintelligible.

119   *bots on't* a plague on it! Bots is a disease of horses.

122   *thy crosses.* Q omits *thy*, which is needed for the metre.
        Wilkins is close to Q here: 'thanking Fortune, that,
        after all her crosses, she had yet given him somewhat
        to repair his fortunes' (page 508).

124   *And though it was mine own.* Something is wrong with
        the text here; *And though* may mean 'even though',
        but the sentence remains confused.

128   *brace* covering for the arms

135   *my father gave* what my father gave me. The con-
        struction is very awkward.

138 *target* armour (properly a shield)

142 *appear* present myself as

144 *pay your bounties* repay your acts of kindness

146 *virtue* valour

150–51 *made up this garment through the rough seams of the waters.* The Second Fisherman sees himself as a tailor; the *seams* are the furrows of the waves.

151–2 *certain condolements, certain vails.* The tailoring image is continued in *vails*, which means the remnants of cloth kept by a tailor after a suit is made up. *Condolements* is a problem word; it has been convincingly argued that it means a share-out, from the root 'dole' (H. M. Hulme, *Explorations in Shakespeare's Language* (1962), pages 279–80).

156 *rapture* seizure, plunder. Q reads 'rupture'; Wilkins gives us 'raptures' (page 508).

157 *building* position, fixed place

159 *courser* (sturdy horse used in tournaments)
delightful full of delight. Q reads 'delight'.

162 *bases* (a kind of skirt worn under armour when riding)

166 *Then honour be but a goal to my will* provided my endeavours have honour alone as their goal

II.2 (stage direction) *Thaisa* (three syllables: 'Ta-eeza')

1 *triumph* tournament

3 *stay* wait for

4 *Return* answer

6 *gat* begat

10 *princes* (men and women of princely rank)

12 *jewels* articles of jewellery (not the precious stones themselves)

14 *entertain* receive

15 *device* emblematic design on a shield

16 (stage direction) This stage direction is based partly on Wilkins, who tells us that each knight entered with his page bearing his shield in front of him. The page

delivered the shield to the Princess, who presented it to the King for his interpretation.

17   *prefer* present

20   *a black Ethiop reaching at the sun.* There is a full study of the devices in *Pericles* in H. Green, *Shakespeare and the Emblem Writers* (1870). Although Green found emblems showing a hand reaching for the sun, he discovered no exact parallel for this. The devices and mottoes of the Third, Fourth, and Fifth Knights were all derived from books of emblems.

21   *word* motto
      Lux tua vita mihi thy light is life to me

27   *Piu per dolcera che per forza.* The text is very muddled here. Q reads 'Pue Per doleera kee per forsa'; this is certainly not Spanish, which would be 'Mas por dulzura que por fuerza'. In Italian, it would be 'Piu per dolcezza che per forza'. The nearest form of the motto which is known is French, 'Plus par doulceur que par force' (More by gentleness than by force). It would be natural to take Q as a corruption of the French version, with *in Spanish* as the reporter's blunder, were it not that Wilkins reads '*Pue per dolcera qui per sforsa*' (page 509). It seems very likely, therefore, that what was heard spoken was a cross between Italian and Spanish, something like what is given here.

29   *wreath of chivalry* (twisted band or chaplet resting on the helmet)

30   *Me pompae provexit apex* the honour of the contest led me on

33   *Qui me alit me extinguit* who feeds me extinguishes me. Compare Shakespeare's Sonnet 73, 'Consumed with that which it was nourished by'.

37   *touchstone* (a piece of smooth black quartz; gold left a particular kind of streak when rubbed along it)

38   *Sic spectanda fides* thus is faithfulness to be tested

43   *In hac spe vivo* in this hope I live. Device and motto seem to be the dramatist's invention.

47–8   *He had need . . . his just commend* one's just assessment of him now, based on his outward appearance, is so low that it is certainly right that he should have higher things in mind

50   *the whipstock* the handle of a whip. The implication is that he has been more of a carter or herdsman than a knight.

55–6   *scan | The outward habit by the inward man.* This is an interesting example of the reporter's mishandling. (See the Introduction, pages 35–6.) Obviously the two terms have become interchanged; the folly is to scan the inward man by the outward habit. But the reporter has sealed up the error in his rhyme-scheme.

58   (stage direction) *mean* humble, poor

II.3.17   *laboured* carefully fashioned
       queen o'th'feast. Compare the way Perdita's 'father' names her 'Mistress o'th'Feast' in *The Winter's Tale*, IV.4.68.

25–6   *Have neither . . . the low despise.* This is awkward and probably corrupt. Q has 'Enuies', and the alteration to *Envied* makes only a minor improvement, leaving us with a difficult antithesis of past and future.

29   *These cates resist me, he but thought upon.* The true reading cannot be retrieved here. *Cates* means 'delicacies'. How they *resist* her is hard to say; she must mean she finds them unpalatable when she thinks of him. Q reads 'not' for *but*. The general sense is given by Wilkins: 'they could not spare so much time to satisfy themselves with the delicacy of their viands, for talking of his praises' (page 510).

38   *Which tells me in what glory.* Q reads 'Which tels in that glory'.

42   *vail* lower

43   *like a glow-worm in the night.* To provide the rhyme, the reporter has muddled the image. (See the Introduction, page 36.) Pericles means that he is like a glow-worm in the daytime, temporarily extinguished.

51   *fill to your mistress' lips.* This awkward phrase is almost certainly a garbling of the original. The King fills a bowl of wine to be sent round the table as a loving-cup, and each knight is to drink to his mistress (Thaisa). The King first drinks the health of his guests.

56   *might countervail* that might be equal to

61   *Who freely give to everyone that come to honour them* (an excessively long line which cannot easily be split up). The allusion is to the ancient doctrine developed by the neo-platonists in relation to the Three Graces, who taught men to honour the gods from whom they would in turn receive benefits.

63   *killed are wondered at* when they are killed you wonder where all that sound came from

64   *entrance* (three syllables: 'enterance') arrival

65   *standing-bowl* (bowl with feet, or stem and base, on which it can stand)

71   *move* anger

78   *pledge him* drink his health (in return)

82   *been* has been
     arts and arms (a standard phrase for all-round talents)

89   *cast* was cast

94   *addressed* accoutred

95   *Will well become.* Either the printer has dropped some words out or the reporter has once again garbled the meaning.

97   *Loud music is too harsh for ladies' heads.* The reporter must have got this wrong. Even if the *Loud music* is the clash of armour, the line is very strained. The passage has been made to seem even more obscure by the frequent assumption that the first dance is by the Knights only. Simonides will not take the excuse that

ladies don't want armoured men for partners, because
they love men in arms(!).

99   *this was well asked* this was well worth suggesting

100   *breathing* exercising

102   *trip* (1) dance; (2) fall into sin

103   *measures* dances

105   *as you would be denied.* The sense has been inverted;
the original must have conveyed 'as you would deny
us'.

106   *Of your fair courtesy.* This can mean either that they
were being denied the pleasure of witnessing his
courtly dancing or that he was denying them in a very
courteous way.

115   *for speeding* to ensure success

II.4.2   *Antiochus from incest lived not free* (an emphatic
juxtaposition of the relation of the two Kings, Simonides and Antiochus, and their daughters)

3   *minding* intending

5   *capital* punishable by death

15   *his* its

16   (stage direction) *two or three* several. Three Lords have
speaking parts.

18   *has respect with him but he* is paid attention to by
Helicanus except Escanes. This hostility towards
Escanes has no before or after.

19   *grieve* offend

23, 25   *griefs* grievances

28   *And know.* Q reads 'Or know'.

31-2   *And be resolved . . . cause to mourn* and be cleared of
doubt whether he's still alive and able to govern us,
or dead, thereby giving us cause to mourn

32   *give's* give us

34   *Whose death indeed's the strongest in our censure* and
indeed his death is in our judgement the more likely
of the two

41 *Try honour's cause.* This is usually but unnecessarily emended to 'For honour's cause'. The disloyalty of the Lords to Pericles is a dishonourable cause; Helicanus suggests they attempt a more honourable devotion.

46 *Further to bear.* Q reads 'To forbeare', seemingly a recollection of the word used twice a few lines before. The reading here was suggested by F. D. Hoeniger.

52 *Whom if you find, and win unto return* and if you find him and persuade him to return

53 *You shall like diamonds sit about his crown* (a mosaic of recollections of II.3.36 and 39)

56 *We with our travels will endeavour it.* The course of this scene seems as confused as a previous encounter between the Lords and Pericles (I.2). Wilkins gives a much more convincing narrative (pages 511–12) in which Helicanus quells a faction who are in 'uncivil and giddy mutiny' in his behalf, and then, assembling the Lords, dispatches a chosen group to search for Pericles.

II.5.10 *One twelve moons* one twelvemonth
wear Diana's livery (remain a virgin)

11–12 *This by the eye . . . not break it.* It is best not to dwell too closely on this barefaced untruth, which will soon make Thaisa appear to the Knights as a shameless and profane vow-breaker. Simonides is strongly characterized as a practical joker. The dramatist knew he would get a laugh at *So, they are well dispatched* (line 14) which would stifle criticism of the King's morals.

17 *nor day nor light.* Compare *Richard II*, V.6.44: 'And never show thy head by day nor light'.

19 *absolute* decided, definite

22 *And will no longer have it be delayed.* The line is clearly inauthentic: the grammar is clumsy and the idea absurd. In the original the King perhaps expressed a hope that the marriage would not be long delayed.

25 *beholding* beholden, indebted

26 *your sweet music this last night.* The very circumstantial description in Wilkins (page 513) of a serenade by Pericles before the entry of Simonides makes it seem likely that this scene should begin with music and a song which Simonides listens to and comments on before the Knights enter.

37 *you must be her master.* In Gower, Pericles becomes schoolmaster to the Princess.

40 *else* if you don't believe it

43 *subtlety* cunning

47 *bent all offices* directed my whole duty

50 *levy* (an unusual usage, having some connexion with the use of the word in 'levy war')

54–6 *That thus disguised ... tender child.* These three blank-verse lines are taken verbatim from Wilkins (page 515), who in this scene follows the action of Q very closely, and often, as here, supplies a fuller and more convincing phrasing of the speeches.

57–8 *Even in his throat ... I return the lie* to anyone except the King who calls me traitor I respond with the charge that he lies in his throat

61 *relished of* were tainted by

63 *to her state* (that is, to honour's kingdom). Wilkins gives 'to his state', that is, Simonides' state, but Q is more likely to be right, maintaining the image of fighting for honour's cause and opposing honour's enemies (lines 62 and 65).

67 *She can witness it.* This inept and truncated rejoinder probably owes something to *Othello*, I.3.169: 'Here comes the lady: let her witness it'. Wilkins gives a fuller version. The King says 'he should prove it otherwise, since by his daughter's hand it there was evident, both his practice [that is, scheming] and her consent therein. Which words were no sooner uttered but Thaisa ... came now in ...' (page 515).

69 *Resolve* assure, clear of doubt

74 *peremptory* self-willed

82   *A straggling Theseus born we know not where.* This line
      from Wilkins, standing out from the monotony of his
      paraphrasing style, proclaims its genuineness and is
      altogether too good to lose, although in adding it to
      what must be an abbreviated and debased version of
      Simonides' speech, there can unfortunately be no hope
      of giving it its proper context. *Straggling* is used of
      one who strays about aimlessly. *Theseus* was the hero
      famous for his far-flung adventures.

         There is another passage of Wilkins which may well
      have been an authentic passage omitted by Q, but the
      compressed report in Q gives us no convenient point
      to insert it: 'Equals to equals, good to good is joined, |
      This not being so, the bavin of your mind,|In rashness
      kindled, must again be quenched' (page 516).

91   *as my life my blood that fosters it* as my life loves the
      blood that nourishes it

III *Chorus*

1   *y-slackèd* quietened
      rout company of revellers
4   *pompous* splendid
5   *eyne* eyes
6   *couches* lies in ambush
8   *their drouth* the dryness of their position
9   *Hymen* (god of marriage)
11   *attent* attentive
12   *briefly* quickly
13   *quaintly* skilfully
      eche eke, add to
14   *plain* make plain
15   *many a dern and painful perch* many a weary mile
      dern dreary
      painful laborious
      perch (a short measure of land)
17   *opposing coigns* opposite corners

21   *stead* contribute to

22   *Fame answering the most strange inquire.* This may be
          corrupt; the sense is that in response to this most
          widespread inquiry rumour gave out that there was a
          mysterious knight in Pentapolis who might be Pericles.

31   *twice six moons.* Compare II.5.10.

32   *dooms* judgements

35   *Y-ravishèd* enraptured

36   *can* (archaic form of ' 'gan')
          sound declare

42   *dole and woe* grief and woe (of their leave-taking)

45–6   *half the flood | Hath their keel cut* they have completed
          half their voyage

47   *grisled* grisly, frightening

51   *well-a-near* alas

52   *travail* labour

55   *nill* will not
          action acting, performance

56   *Conveniently* fittingly

57   *Which might not what by me is told* which is not the case
          for the narrative I have related so far

60   *appears to speak* appears and speaks

I.1.1   *The god of this great vast* (Neptune). Many editions
          read 'Thou god …' to conform with the vocative
          thou in the next line. But Q may well be correct in
          making Pericles change from an indirect plea to
          direct address as he turns from Neptune to Aeolus.
          vast waste, desolate expanse
          surges waves

2–3   *thou that hast | Upon the winds command, bind them in
          brass.* Aeolus was the god of the winds; he came to be
          associated with Vulcan the blacksmith, and hence the
          strange command *bind them in brass.*

6   *nimble, sulphurous.* These adjectives are applied to
          lightning in *King Lear*, II.4.160 and III.2.4.

7   *Thou storm, venomously.* Q prints 'then storme
        venomously,'. The image is of the storm as a huge
        swollen toad spitting its poison from the skies.

9–10   *Is as a whisper in the ears of death,* | *Unheard* can no
        more be heard than can a whisper in the ear of one
        who has just died

10   *Lucina* (goddess of childbirth, already mentioned in
        connexion with the birth of Antiochus's daughter,
        I.1.9)

16   *conceit* capacity to understand

19   *do not assist the storm.* The same phrase is used much
        less awkwardly at the beginning of *The Tempest*
        (I.1.13–14), when the Boatswain tells the courtiers to
        keep below: 'You mar our labour. . . . You do assist
        the storm.' *The Tempest* dates from about 1611, three
        years later than *Pericles*.

26   *Use honour.* The meaning is not clear. The usual
        emendation, 'Vie honour', is very strained.

27   *for this charge* for the sake of this baby for whom you
        now have the responsibility

29   *conditions* way of life

34   *Poor inch of nature!* This is supplied from Wilkins,
        whose version runs as follows: ' . . . he taking to kiss,
        and pitying it with these words, "Poor inch of nature",
        quoth he, "thou art as rudely welcome to the world as
        ever princess' babe was, and hast as chiding a nativity
        as fire, air, earth, and water can afford thee" ' (page
        519).

35–6   *Even at the first . . . find here* at the very beginning of
        your life, you have lost more than you can ever replace,
        however much you gain in the rest of your life. *Portage*
        is a problem word; it has something to do with trans-
        port or cargo, hence perhaps 'voyage through life' or
        'possessions, endowments'. It is possible that the word
        is a misprint or misreading of 'partage', meaning 'a
        share in life'.

39   *flaw* squall

43   *bolins* bowlines (ropes for steadying the sails in a strong wind)

43–5   *Thou wilt not ... But sea-room.* There is again a close parallel with the opening of *The Tempest* (I.1.6–7), where the Boatswain also addresses the storm: 'Blow till thou burst thy wind, if room enough'.

45   *But sea-room* just give us room to manoeuvre, away from a lee shore
    an if

45–6   *cloudy billow* (the spray from the waves creating a mist like a cloud)

48   *works high* rages, is turbulent

50   *That's your superstition.* The belief that a dead body brought harm to a ship was widespread and long-lasting.

52   *still* always

55   (stage direction) *She reveals the body of Thaisa* (not in Q). Lychorida probably drew back a curtain at the rear of the stage. In the same way, perhaps, Cleon revealed the tomb of Marina in IV.4, and Helicanus revealed Pericles in V.1.

60   *in the ooze.* Q reads 'in oare'. The accepted emendation (given here) is held to be justified by the parallel with *The Tempest*, III.3.102: 'my son i'th'ooze is bedded'; but it is almost certainly wrong. It is retained here because the line is now a part of English poetry and the true reading seems inaccessible. In *The Tempest*, the picture is of a corpse lying in the mud. Here the picture is of casting a coffin into the deep sea to lie at last on the sea-bed *with simple shells*. The number of errors by the compositor in this part of the play shows that the copy gave the printer much difficulty. The sort of phrase needed here is 'to the deep' or 'in the flood'.

61–2   *for a monument upon thy bones, | And e'er-remaining lamps* instead of a monument placed over your grave

and ever-burning votive lights. Q reads 'ayre remayn-
ing' and it is uncertain whether the true reading is
e'er-remaining or *'aye-remaining'*.

62   *belching* spouting

63   *humming water must o'erwhelm thy corpse.* This
beautiful line was remembered by Milton as he wrote
Lycidas; at line 157 he originally wrote 'under the
humming tide', and later changed it to 'under the
whelming tide'.

       humming murmuring

69   *Suddenly* immediately

71   *bitumed* made watertight with bitumen, or pitch

73   FIRST SAILOR. Q and all editions give this and the
next sailor's speech to the Second Sailor. But Pericles'
change of address to *Mariner* in the preceding speech,
coupled with the clear inference that he is talking to
the ship's master, makes it obvious that here it is the
first and senior of the sailors who speaks.

75   *thy course for Tyre* your course, which is now towards
Tyre

76   *By break of day.* Many hundreds of miles separate
Tarsus from Ephesus (see the map on page 6). It is
impossible that on the morning after the storm
Thaisa's body should be washed up in Ephesus, and
Pericles' ship reach Tarsus. Moreover, if the gale was
from the north (III Chorus 47; IV.1.52), a ship sail-
ing from Pentapolis to Tyre would not have been
driven north towards Ephesus and Tarsus.

81   *presently* at once

III.2.1–10   The action at the beginning of the scene is confused.
Q gives only one servant entering with Cerimon, but it
is clear that in lines 7–10 Cerimon addresses two
separate people. There is also the problem of *these poor
men* in the third line. It seems best to bring on two

servants and to suppose that *these poor men* are ship-wrecked people off stage, to whom Philemon is ordered to bring a fire and food.

8   *There's nothing can be ministered to nature* there's no medicine that can be given as a help to nature

13   *bleak upon* exposed to

14   *Shook as the earth did quake.* The verse in this scene is erratically and irregularly divided in Q. Although it is possible with a good deal of ingenuity to redivide it into a reasonable pattern of iambic blank-verse lines, we are left with many short lines (as here) and other irregularities which indicate that we are dealing with an incomplete and inaccurate report and not an author-ized manuscript. See the Introduction, pages 35-9.
    as as if

15   *principals* main beams

16   *Pure* sheer

19   *husbandry* industrious habits

21   *tire* appurtenances, possessions

24   *conversant* (accented on the first syllable)
    pain toil, effort

26   *cunning* skill

31   *physic* medical science
    secret hidden, obscure

32   *turning o'er* examining carefully

33   *practice* practical investigations

34   *To me and to my aid.* He not only knows these infusions; he knows how to make them assist in healing.
    infusions liquid extracts

35   *vegetives* plants, herbs

38   *A more content in course of true delight.* Weakness of this kind suggests a lapse in the reporting.

40   *tie my pleasure up in silken bags* confine my pleasures to the miserly acquisition or retention of wealth

41   *To please the fool and death.* The only ones who can find the pleasure he has spoken of are fools, and death (who in the end inherits the wealth). There may be an

allusion to the figures in the traditional pictures of the Dance of Death.

42   *Ephesus* (on the west coast of Asia Minor; renowned for its great temple to Diana)

43   *creatures* dependants acknowledging they owe life to you

44   *not* not only

45   *still* always

47   *As time shall never –*. A final word is missing here. The interruption of the entry of the Servants with a chest makes it likely that in stage performance the Second Gentleman was never allowed to finish his speech.

     (stage direction) *Enter two or three with a chest.* One of these men, who has a speaking part, is called Servant when he speaks. So many parts must have been doubled in this play that it hardly matters 'identifying' this group, but they would probably be the same actors whom Cerimon sent on their way as servants at the beginning of the scene.

54   *constraint* (meaningless in the context and probably an error)

58   *Soft!* gently! (As they begin to *Wrench it open*, Cerimon perceives there is something special about the chest.)

61   *corse* corpse

63   *cloth of state* regal fabric (properly, the canopy which goes over a chair of state)

     balmed anointed

     entreasured laid up as a precious thing in a treasury

64   *A passport too!* This phrase, understandably but unfortunately, raises a laugh in the modern theatre. One ingenious suggestion is that, since a passport describes a person, Cerimon means 'a document describing the contents'.

65   *Apollo* (the god both of medicine and eloquence)

     perfect me in make me perfect in understanding

67   *drives a-land* is driven (that is, drifts) ashore

69   *all our mundane cost* the value of our entire world

75   *That ever cracks* that is broken for ever

       tonight (the night which has just ended)

82–5 *I have … health.* This passage is taken (with the omission of one small phrase) from Wilkins (page 522). Q at this point seems quite wrong: 'I heard of an *Egiptian* that had 9. howers lien dead, | Who was by good applyaunce recouered.' See the Account of the Text, page 198.

86   *Well said* well done

87   *rough and woeful music.* The epithet *rough* is very strange, and some editors read 'still' because of Wilkins's phrase, 'command some still music to sound' (page 523). But, since *rough* is such an unusual word in the context, it is most unlikely to be a reporter's error; substitutions tend towards the more expected and conventional words. There may, however, be a compositor's misreading. If *rough* is correct, we have to imagine that some very eerie and unusual music accompanied the semi-miracle of the raising of Thaisa; or it is just possible that Cerimon is speaking deprecatingly of the poor resources he has for music.

89   *The viol once more! How thou stirrest, thou block!* The music ceases; it is essential for the recovery of Thaisa, and Cerimon, busy about the body, is moved to irritation by the slowness of a servant to obey his order to tell the musicians to strike up again.

93   *entranced* in a trance, unconscious

95   *The heavens, through you, increase our wonder* your skill must be heaven-sent, and increases our wonder at the power of the gods

100   *water* lustre

104   *Where am I? Where's my lord? What world is this?* This is straight from Gower: 'She spake and said: Where am I? | Where is my lord? What world is this?'.

109   *is mortal* would be fatal

110   *Aesculapius* (god of healing)

III.3.2   *My twelve months are expired*. Pericles means the twelve months allowed by the lords of Tyre to give their prince a chance to reappear (see III Chorus 31).

3   *litigious peace* peace marred by contention

3–5   *You and your lady . . . upon you!* when you have had all the gratitude my heart is capable of, it will not be a sufficient return; may the gods supply what is wanting

5–7   *Your shakes of fortune . . . wonderingly on us* the shocks of fortune which you have suffered, though they continue to afflict you murderously, touch us also and amaze us. *Shakes* means 'violent shocks' (as of an earthquake); *haunt* was regularly used of the recurrent visitation of a disease; *wonderingly* means 'with wonder'. Editors have completely rewritten this passage by substituting 'shafts' for *shakes*, 'hurt' for *haunt*, and 'woundingly' for *wonderingly*.

13   *for* because

20   *neglection* neglect

21   *the common body* the people

25   *To the end of generation* till humanity ceases to exist

29   *Unscissored shall this hair of mine remain*. The compositor of Q showed both the difficulty he had with the handwriting in the copy and his own ingenuity by printing 'vnsisterd shall this heyre of mine remayne'! Wilkins (page 524) reads 'vowing solemnly . . . his head should grow unscissored . . . till he had married his daughter'.

30   *Though I show will in't* though my resolution may seem wilful

36   *the masked Neptune*. This may express the hope that Neptune will mask his malevolence.

III.4.3   *character* handwriting

6   *bearing time* time of child-bearing. Q has 'learning time'. Most editions give 'eaning', a term used of sheep.

9 *I ne'er shall see again.* Some words, showing that Thaisa believes her husband has been drowned, seem to have been lost here.

10 *A vestal livery* the clothes (and hence the life) of a vestal virgin (dedicated to chastity and the preservation of the sacred fire in the temple of the goddess Vesta)

14 *date* term of life

IV Chorus

2 *to* in accordance with

4 *there's* there as

   votaress votary (woman devoted to the worship of a saint or god)

8 *music's letters* the art or learning of music. But probably the original text spoke of music and letters (that is, literature).

10 *heart and place.* Q gives 'art and place'. The emendation is not very convincing.

12 *wrack* wreck

15–16 *And in this kind . . . full-grown wench.* There is obvious corruption here, besides the difficulty of the phrasing.

18 *Hight* is called

21 *sleded* (a very rare word) fine-drawn

23 *needle* (probably pronounced 'neel'; compare *neele* at V Chorus 5)

24 *cambric* (fine white linen)

26 *night-bird* nightingale

27 *still* always

   records sings

   with moan plaintively

28 *with rich and constant pen.* This presumably refers to writing hymns.

29 *Vail* do homage

31 *absolute* perfect

32 *dove of Paphos* (white dove sacred to Venus, whose town was Paphos, in Cyprus)

33   *Vie* offer in competition
35   *darks* darkens, subdues
38   *present* immediate
41   *her vile thoughts to stead* to assist her vile designs
44   *pregnant* compliant
45   *Prest* ready
       event outcome
47–8   *Only I carried wingèd time | Post on the lame feet of my*
       rhyme my narrative went faster than time, in spite of
       my halting verses

IV.1   The verse in this scene is printed in Q almost entirely
           as prose. The redivision is bound to be unsatisfactory
           because the reported text is incomplete; any editorial
           rearrangement leaves a number of fragmentary lines,
           and there will always be disagreement about which are
           the complete lines of verse.
3   *soon* quickly
5–6   *inflaming love in thy bosom, | Inflame too nicely.* Q reads
           'in flaming, thy loue bosome, enflame too nicelie'.
           Once again, one has little conviction that the reading
           here offered is the true version of a corrupt passage.
6   *nicely* fastidiously
13   *Tellus* (the earth)
           weed garment (of flowers)
14   *green* (the green grass of the grave)
16   *carpet* tapestry
20   *Whirring* whirling
21   *keep* remain
24   *Have you a nurse of me* make me your nurse
           favour appearance
26   *On the sea-margent* by the edge (margin) of the sea. Q
           reads 'ere the sea marre it', which cannot be right.
27   *quick* enlivening
28   *pierces and sharpens the stomach* penetrates (and does
           good) to the digestion and increases the appetite

33   *With more than foreign heart* as if I were of your family
35   *Our paragon to all reports* one who according to all the
reports he has received is a model of excellence
38   *to your best courses* of what was best for you
39   *Reserve* preserve
47   *warrant* promise
49   *softly* slowly
54   *galling* chafing
55   *haling* pulling
61   *ladder-tackle* rope ladder in the rigging
62   *canvas-climber* sailor climbing to trim the sails
      wolt out? wilt thou out? (The application is obscure.)
63   *dropping* dripping-wet
77   *law* (an exclamation used to strengthen a statement,
rather like 'indeed')
86   *well-favoured* of a good appearance
95   *Half-part* half. (He claims his share.)
97   *roguing* feloniously wandering
      Valdes. The name may have been suggested by
Pedro de Valdes, a Spanish admiral captured by
Drake.

V.2   (stage direction) *the three Bawds.* A bawd is someone
concerned in the brothel trade – chiefly in obtaining
customers or prostitutes. The bawds in the play are
designated Pander, Boult, and Bawd. The Pander and
the Bawd are man and wife, and Boult (a phallic name)
is their man.
3   *Mytilene* (the chief city of the island of Lesbos, off the
west coast of Asia Minor)
4   *mart* market time
11–12   *If there be not a conscience to be used in every trade* if we
don't use that conscience which ought to be used in
every trade. The Pander's idea of conscience, or moral
conduct, is to spare no expense in acquiring new
whores.

15   *to eleven, and brought them down again* to eleven years old, then reduced them to service in the brothel

18   *sodden* rotten. The literal meaning is 'stewed', an appropriate word for one worn out by disease in the 'stews', as brothels were called; the same pun occurs in *Troilus and Cressida*, III.1.40.

19   *there's two unwholesome.* Most editions alter this to 'they're too unwholesome'; but the point of the grim humour is that on such evidence as the death of a client you could say that two of the three *are* unwholesome.

19–20 *o' conscience* (on my conscience) I'm sure

20   *Transylvanian.* Transylvania lay in what is now Hungary.

22   *pooped him.* 'Poop' was a low word for the female genitals. This use of the verb is scarcely translatable: 'did for him by infecting him venereally'.

24   *chequins* (gold coins)

25   *proportion* portion, share
      give over give up the trade

26   *get* make money

28–9 *our credit ... the danger* reputation doesn't roll in as easily as the profit, and the profit doesn't measure up to the danger

31   *hatched* half shut. (A hatch is the lower half of a divided door.)

33   *strong* (as an argument)

34   *sorts* classes of people

36–7 *Neither is our profession any trade; it's no calling* and the life we follow is no recognized trade or vocation

41   *gone through* bargained
      piece piece of flesh (a contemptuous term for woman as sex object; but compare IV.6.109, *a piece of virtue*)

42   *earnest* deposit

43   *qualities* accomplishments

45–6 *There's no farther necessity of qualities can make her be refused.* This confusion may be Boult's or the reporter's.

The sentence is a joining of the halves of alternative statements: 'There's no farther necessity of qualities to make her acceptable' and 'There's no deficiency of qualities to make her be refused.'

48   *be bated* get it reduced (literally, 'be reduced')
      doit (a Dutch coin worth half a farthing; hence 'the least amount')
50   *presently* immediately
52   *entertainment* reception of clients
62–3 *had not o'erboard | Thrown me.* The more comprehensible construction would be 'did not . . . throw me' (following *Alack that*).
68   *light* fallen
76   *difference of all complexions* variety of men of every disposition and appearance
85   *by men* by means of men
86–7 *stir . . . up* rouse, stimulate
88   *cried her* announced her for sale
89   *almost to the number of her hairs* almost as far as numbering the hairs of her head
100   *cowers i'the hams* has crooked legs, walks in crouching fashion
101   *Veroles* (from the French *vérole*, 'pox'; '*Verollus*' in Q)
102   *offered to* made a move to
      cut a caper perform a jump kicking the feet together in the air
105–6 *he brought his disease hither* he already had venereal disease when he first came here
106   *repair* renew
106–7 *in our shadow* under our roof
107   *crowns of the sun* French crowns (euphemism for the effects of syphilis). Q reads 'in' for *of*.
109   *this sign* (the beauty of Marina)
116   *mere* absolute
118   *take her home* make her aware of the situation
119   *present* immediate

121–3   *your bride ... with warrant* even a lawful bride is bashful at first

124–6   *if I have bargained for the joint – Thou mayst cut a morsel off the spit.* This dark exchange stuck in Wilkins's memory, but he put it later (page 537), at the point when Lysimachus leaves, and he may well be right.

131–2   *spend thou . . . we have.* The reporter is almost certainly confused in creating a second, repetitive, unnecessary advertising tour by Boult. Presumably this passage belongs to the earlier commission to go out into the town.

132   *You'll lose nothing by custom* (the more clients, the greater the commission)

133   *piece* excellent product (as in 'masterpiece'). There is a pun on the disreputable meaning (see line 41).

136–7   *thunder . . . eels.* It was a common belief that eels were roused from the mud by thunder. There is a bawdy innuendo here.

IV.3.11   *drunk to him* toasted him in the poison

12   *fact* crime. Q reads 'face'.

14–15   *Nurses are not the Fates . . . preserve.* Q makes no sense at all (see Collations list 1a). The nineteenth-century emendation given here (it was recently discovered by J. C. Maxwell) is a convincing restoration: nurses are not the Fates to decide the length of life; to foster a child is not to preserve it for ever.

17   *play the impious innocent* impiously play the innocent. *Impious* means undutiful to Dionyza. All editions emend to 'play the pious innocent', a phrase given by Wilkins, which is clearly a failure to take the bold oxymoron of the text. Dionyza's idea of piety relates entirely to the family; see lines 35–9.

18   *attribute* reputation

22–3   *The petty wrens . . . open this* (an allusion to folk-tales in which murders are revealed by birds)

27 *prime* original, previous. Q reads 'prince'.

28 *courses* tributary streams. To Dionyza's taunt about his *noble strain*, Cleon retorts that to approve of the deed when it was done, let alone consent to it beforehand, would be enough to deny the nobility of one's origins.

31 *distain* cast a stain on, overshadow. Q reads 'disdaine'.

34 *blurted at* treated contemptuously. To 'blurt' is to make a derisive noise with the lips.
  malkin slut

35 *Not worth the time of day* not worth saying 'good day' to

37 *You not your child well loving* you who do not love your own child properly

38 *greets me* presents itself pleasingly to me
  kindness natural affection

42 *yet* still

46–8 *like the harpy ... thine eagle's talons.* The harpy was a fabulous beast with a woman's face and torso and a bird's wings and claws. The text seems corrupt; the original must have included something about luring before seizing.

49–50 *one that superstitiously ... kills the flies.* The passage is obscure and perhaps corrupt. Apparently Dionyza is continuing her argument that her crime is natural, like winter killing the flies.

.4 This Gower chorus differs from all those which precede it by being in heroic couplets, ten syllables to a line, instead of octosyllabics. There is also less 'medievalism' in the language here, and an even greater insistence on the fiction of the play. See the Introduction, pages 40–41.

1 *waste* lay waste, annihilate
  leagues. A league is about three miles.

2 *cockles* cockle-shells. The shallow coracle-type boat is probably meant.

2   *have and wish but for't* have something just by wishing for it

3–4 *Making to take your imagination | From bourn to bourn.* This is obscure and perhaps corrupt; Q reads 'our' for *your*. It seems best to understand *Making* in its medieval sense of composing poetry, here used intransitively: 'writing poetry in order to take your imagination' etc.

4   *bourn* frontier

10   *thwarting* crossing
     wayward contrary, hostile

14   *you bear in mind.* We have heard nothing of this.

18   *his pilot.* Q reads 'this Pilat'. The passage is obscure and perhaps corrupt. A not very convincing interpretation is that Pericles' boat goes as swift as thought, and if the audience use the same pilot, they will be able to keep up with him.

20   *first* already

21   *motes* (floating specks of dust in a beam of light)

22   (stage direction) *Cleon shows Pericles the tomb.* See the note to III.1.55.
     passion grief

23   *suffer by foul show* be abused by false presentation

24   *This borrowed passion stands for true old woe.* Gower makes a contrast between Dionyza, acting a *foul show* and exhibiting grief where there is none, and the actor taking the part of Pericles, whose exhibition of grief (*borrowed passion*) represents a genuine emotion.

29   *He bears* (within him)

30   *his mortal vessel* (his body)

31   *wit* know

38–43 *Marina . . . shores of flint.* The metre of the epitaph changes into ten-syllable lines, and there is a simultaneous descent into near-nonsense, as bad as anything in the cobbled verse of the first two acts. Something went wrong with the report at this point, and the need to observe rhyme has led to a ludicrous reconstruction.

39	*Thetis* (a sea-nymph; here, as often, confused with Tethys, wife of Oceanus)
47–8	*bear his courses . . . Fortune* allow Fortune to conduct his life
49	*well-a-day* grief
51	*Mytilene* (three syllables rhyming with *then* here, and with *din* at V.2.8)

V.5.7	*vestals* vestal virgins
9	*rutting* fornication

V.6.4	*Priapus* (god of fertility). In Laurence Twine's version of the story, a lewd statue of Priapus stands in the brothel.
6	*her fitment* what is fit and proper for her to do. The word is not recorded elsewhere with this meaning.
6, 7	*me* (the ethical dative, more obvious in the second instance than the first)
6	*kindness* natural acts of goodness
9	*cheapen* bargain for
12	*cavalleria* (Italian) chivalry, body of knights
13	*green-sickness* (anaemia in young women, hence 'sickly immaturity')
15	*Lysimachus*. The name is not in the sources, but it is found in the story in Plutarch referred to in the note to I.3.4–6.
16	*lown* (often spelt 'loon') lowbred fellow
18	*how* how much
19	*to bless* (an odd phrasing which may indicate a corruption)
22	*resorters* habitual visitors, customers
22–3	*How now, wholesome iniquity have you*. Many editors put a comma after *iniquity*, instead of after *have you*, thus making the phrase a term of address for the

Bawd. The punctuation of Q, followed here, indicates
that Lysimachus is inquiring for a healthy whore.

23　*deal withal* have dealings with

24　*surgeon* doctor

27　*the deeds of darkness* copulation

29　*knows what 'tis to say well enough* is very good at putting
it into words (said ironically)

32　*if she had but –* (– a thorn; the innuendo is clearer in
the Elizabethan form of the proverb, 'No roses without
prickles')

35–6　*That dignifies ... to be chaste* modesty dignifies a
bawd's reputation, and causes a number of immoral
people to be thought chaste

40–41　*she would serve after a long voyage at sea.* A coarse
expression of admiration: she's just the girl a sex-
starved sailor would be delighted to meet. I think it is
unlikely that Lysimachus pretends not to be impressed, and means that she would be all right for an
undiscriminating sailor.

50–53　*a man ... I know not.* The Bawd says she is under
certain obligations to Lysimachus (presumably for not
closing her brothel down). Marina replies that all
people are bound to their governors by ties of obedi-
ence, but neither obligations nor ties prove the honour-
ableness of the prince.

54　*virginal fencing* verbal fencing to maintain virginity

59–60　*paced ... work her to your manage* (the vocabulary of
training horses)

71　*gamester* whore, woman inclined to 'the sport'

77　*parts* qualities

81　*herb-woman* woman who sells herbs

82　From this point Q gives us a text which, even without
the evidence of Wilkins's much more expansive report,
we could tell was abbreviated and seriously garbled.
It is a great misfortune that the authentic version of
this crucial exchange has been irretrievably lost. See
the Introduction, pages 21–6.

85-6 *my authority . . . upon thee.* Wilkins gives a much fuller version than this. Lysimachus 'began to be more rough with her', saying his authority could either overlook faults or punish them at his pleasure, 'which displeasure of mine thy beauty shall not privilege thee from' (page 535).

89 *If put upon you* if the position of honour was bestowed upon you

91 *Some more. Be sage.* The whole line is unconvincing and probably truncated, but, if it is a reflection of the original, the great eighteenth-century editor Edmond Malone must be right that it is said with a sneer: 'Proceed with your fine moral discourse.'

91-8 *For me . . . purer air!* In Wilkins's novel, Marina is given three long speeches of explanation, pleading, and persuasion, instead of the two brief and halting speeches given in Q. First she explains her history. Lysimachus is sceptical, answering with the rough speech corresponding to lines 82-6. Marina then makes a long and passionate speech, appealing to Lysimachus's honour, represented in Q by the three lines 88-90. Lysimachus replies with a speech corresponding to lines 73-4. With her third long speech, beginning with the sharp rejoinder given by Q at lines 75-6, Marina throws herself on Lysimachus's mercy and kneels before him. While Wilkins's language is only at moments Shakespearian, and indeed omits the two or three authentic-sounding phrases found in Q, the general structure of the scene is much more convincing than that of Q. See the Introduction, pages 22-3.

101-2 *Had I brought . . . had altered it.* In his next speech, Lysimachus adds *I came with no ill intent.* Although the dramatic conventions of testing young women by a pretence of threatening behaviour allowed situations which we find unacceptable, it is impossible to take these lines as implying that Lysimachus has for some inscrutable reason only been playing with Marina. See the Introduction, pages 23–4. Nothing else in the play can support such a suggestion. The diametrically opposite position is given in Wilkins (page 536): 'I hither came with thoughts intemperate, foul and deformed, the which your pains so well have laved that they are now white ... for my part, who hither came but to have paid the price, a piece of gold, for your virginity, now give you twenty to relieve your honesty.'

There are four possible explanations of the discrepancy between Q and Wilkins:

(a) Q gives the correct version and Wilkins got it wrong; Lysimachus never intended to seduce Marina.

(b) Wilkins gives the correct version, which was misunderstood by the reporter.

(c) This part of the play was altered between the time Wilkins saw it and the time of the reconstruction of the Q text.

(d) Lysimachus's words in Q do not necessarily mean that he was only pretending an assault on Marina's virtue.

The first explanation is unacceptable for reasons argued at length in the Introduction (pages 22–6). All the support necessary for a deception of this kind is absent, and such a deception would make nonsense of a major issue in the play. The third explanation is not impossible; someone (not the author) might have tampered with the boldness of the original concept of reforming a sinful Lysimachus. But the true explanation probably lies between (b) and (c). Wilkins is basically correct in reporting a humbled and ashamed Lysimachus confessing his errors. But part of the apology may have been that his mind was not corrupted though his actions were thoughtless; that he did not come with the ill intent of destroying a woman's being, that he came rather for a moment's pleasure, as he then saw it. In preserving the apologia and omitting the confession, Q has arguably altered the balance of the play.

103   *Persever* (accented on the second syllable)

106   *be you thoughten.* This is not English, and can hardly be the true reading.

108   *savour* smell

109   *piece* outstanding example

116   *doorkeeper.* The word was commonly used for a whoremaster or procurer.

119   The language of Q improves immediately on the entry of Boult. But it is clear, from repetitions and 'fill-in' phrases, and the dubious sequence of the speeches, that we are still faced with a reconstructed text.

121   *cope* sky

124   *Whither would you have me?* This is more or less repeated at line 151 below. As the following speech by Boult has the same tenor in each place it is possible that this exchange between Marina and Boult does not belong here, and ought to be in the later place.

140   *Crack the glass of her virginity.* The image seems to be of a glass vessel, rigid and brittle, rather than of the self-regarding looking-glass.

145   *conjures* uses magic to invoke supernatural aid

148–9   *dish of chastity with rosemary and bays.* The Bawd sees Marina as a meal, garnished with herbs, for Boult.

154   *thing* (with a quibble on *thing* as the female organ)

159   *better thee in their command* have the advantage over you of being in command

161   *pained'st* most tormented

163   *custrel* knave, base fellow

164   *Tib* low woman

165   *fisting* punching

174   *common shores* (beaches or river-banks used for dumping rubbish; or open sewers)

175   *by indenture* (as an apprentice)

178   *own a name too dear* possess too high a reputation (that

is, the baboon wouldn't lower himself to Boult's profession)

188   *Prove* if you find

189   *groom* menial

V *Chorus*

This chorus is in another new metre, ten-syllable lines rhyming alternately. Apart from uncertainties, especially at the end, Q seems to give a reliable text. There is an immediate deterioration when the bustle of stage action begins at V.1.

5   *Deep clerks she dumbs* she reduces men of profound learning to silence

     neele needle

8   *inkle* linen thread or yarn

     twin (Q: 'Twine'). This and the previous line have the same tenor: Marina's embroidery is a near-relation of the objects it represents.

19   *sable* black

22   *heavy* sorrowful

23–4   *what is done . . . be discovered.* This is Gower's customary indication that we are now to change from narrative report to stage action, but the language is clumsy. Perhaps the meaning is 'What takes place will be shown in stage action, and we would show more if it were feasible.'

V.1   Both the verse and the stage business of the opening of the scene seem muddled and awkward, and we are reminded of similar examples in the early acts of the reporter's difficulties in reconstructing scenes which began with a lot of coming and going by minor characters (for example I.2).

1   SAILOR OF TYRE. The designation of the sailors and the division of the speeches between them is editorial.

Q calls them '2. *Saylers*' and seems arbitrary in allotting the speeches.

resolve you clear up your difficulties

9   *some* someone

16   *Neptune's triumphs* public shows in tribute to Neptune

24   *prorogue* prolong

25   *Upon what ground is* what is the cause of

      distemperature unsettlement, disturbance

30   *bootless* unavailing

32   (stage direction) *Helicanus ... a couch.* Q has no direction for the 'discovery' of Pericles. Presumably he lies within the curtained space already used for the showing of Thaisa's body and Marina's tomb.

43   *chosen* choice, outstanding

44   *battery* assault

      ports gates (of his senses). Q has 'parts'.

49   (stage direction) *Exit Lord.* There is no stage direction in Q, and no order for Marina to be fetched. Editors suggest that Lysimachus whispers to the Lord, but since the Lord has himself suggested that Marina ough to be present, a nod would do.

53   *That for our gold we may provision have.* There is some confusion between this passage and the end of the scene, where the question of provisioning is taken up again. See line 256.

55   *for* because of

56   *most just God.* The text of Q is so uneasy in this scene that one cannot put much reliance on this sudden change from the plural gods of the play to a single providence, but it may be authentic. Many editions alter *God* to 'gods'.

57   *graff* grafted plant

59   *at large* in full

64   *presence* appearance, bearing

67   *Came of a gentle kind* that she came from a well-born family. *Noble stock* duplicates *gentle kind*, and the repetition seems flat and inauthentic.

69 *all goodness that consists in beauty* (addressed to Marina) who are all the goodness which dwells in beauty

70 *Expect even here* (imperative: the object of the verb is the clause beginning *Thy sacred physic*)

71 *prosperous* able to bring good results (as in 'a prosperous gale')
  artificial feat skilful action

78 (stage direction) *Marina sings.* Q reads '*The Song*'; the text is lost.

81 *Hail, sir! My lord, lend ear.* She must have said more than this.

82 (stage direction) *He pushes her away.* Q has no direction here. See line 99, *You would not do me violence*, and line 126, *when I did push thee back*. Wilkins, probably following Twine rather than stage action, says he 'struck her on the face' (page 543).

88 *wayward* contrary
  malign deal malignantly with

92 *awkward casualties* adverse happenings

94–5 *there is . . . he speak.* A presentiment excites a flush in her face and prompts her to wait.

101 *What countrywoman?* of what country are you?

103 *mortally* humanly

104 *No other than I appear* (not a spirit)

105 *deliver weeping* unburden my grief in tears

108 *square brows* high and broad forehead
  stature height

110 *cased as richly.* Compare III.2.97–100.

111 *In pace another Juno.* A goddess was known by her walk, so Virgil said (*Aeneid*, I, 405).

112–13 *Who starves . . . gives them speech.* Compare *Antony and Cleopatra*, II.2.241–2: 'she makes them hungry | Where most she satisfies.'

117 *to owe* by owning them

119 *disdained in the reporting* scorned as soon as uttered

123 *thy relation* what you relate

125 *friends* relations

128 *descending* descent

130 *tossed from wrong to injury* (one of the few phrases of this scene preserved also in Wilkins (page 543), who is very sketchy at this point)

131 *thought'st*. Q reads 'thoughts', indicating the pronunciation.

132 *opened* made plain

136 *my endurance* what I have endured

138–9 *Patience ... out of act.* Marina is seen by Pericles as a statue of Patience (compare *Twelfth Night*, II.4.113–14: 'Patience on a monument, | Smiling at grief') who sees unmoved the vicissitudes of kings and kingdoms, and who, by her quiet acceptance, defeats the worst that calamity can do.

154 *Motion as well?* Q reads 'Motion well,'. The meaning is disputed. The reading adopted here, meaning 'and do you have the power of moving as well?', fits in with the preceding *working pulse*, but it can be no more than a guess at the lost true reading.

160 *Delivered weeping* related in tears (a tell-tale repetition of Pericles' words in line 105)

162 *withal* with

163 *buried* who is dead and buried

168 *By the syllable* in every word

174–7 *And having wooed ... Mytilene.* There is a severe breakdown in the quality of the reporting at this point, and to attempt to straighten the grammar out is compounding a felony.

175 *drawn.* In the context, this can mean either 'approached' or 'drawn his sword', but it is possible that in the original there was a phrase about Leonine being *drawn* in the sense of 'incited' or 'induced'.

178 *Whither will you have me?* what is the goal of your questioning? (But this is one of the reporter's stock phrases. See the note to IV.6.124.)

181 *be* be alive

185 *or what is like to be.* This looks like an inauthentic

'fill-in'; it certainly weakens the force of the question.

188   *Speaks* who speaks

190   *still.* This probably but not certainly has the force of 'always'.

194   *O'erbear* overwhelm

196   *Thou that beget'st him that did thee beget.* This line is the key to the play, and perhaps to the whole group of Shakespeare's late Romances. The daughter gives new life to the father when they truly discover each other in a bond of love. The paradox is the ancient paradox of Christianity, in which God the father becomes the son of his own daughter, a virgin. (See E. R. Curtius, *European Literature and the Latin Middle Ages*, translated by Willard R. Trask, 1953, page 42.) The relationship of Pericles and Marina is strongly contrasted with that of Antiochus and his daughter, bound together in fruitless lust (*He's father, son, and husband mild . . .* , I.1.69).

206–9   *as in the rest . . . thy father.* This passage is badly corrupted and even with the help of liberal emendation the original cannot be recovered. The general sense is 'If you are able to tell me my queen's name with the same divine accuracy which you have shown in the rest of your story, you become the heir of my kingdom and the bringer of new life to me.'

212–13   *who did end | The minute I began.* Very similar words occur at the point in *The Winter's Tale* (V.3.45) when Perdita speaks of her long-lost mother: 'Dear queen, that ended when I but began'.

215   *Mine own* she is my own

216   *as she should have been* as it was made out she was

218   *justify in knowledge* recognize by reason of full knowledge

223   *I am wild in my beholding* there is a kind of delirium in my perceiving

229   *The music of the spheres.* The turning of the supposed concentric spheres of the universe was held to produce

celestial music. We cannot say for certain whether Shakespeare intended some music to be heard in performance.

233 *nips* (a most unexpected word in this context, but too original for a reporter)

236–8 *Well, my companion friends ... remember you.* This looks very much like reporter's tack.

239–48 Diana's speech was probably rhymed throughout in the original.

244 *call* speak out loudly

245 *repetition to the life* a faithful report

246 *Or* either

249 *argentine* clad in silver (the colour of virginity)

254 *blown.* Though literally this means 'inflated by the wind', the sense here is probably 'much blown'; the sails have seen a lot of service in Pericles' voyages.

  Eftsoons later on

2.5 *aptly* readily

8 *Mytilene.* See the note to IV.4.51.

12 *Till he had done his sacrifice* (referring now to Pericles)

13 *bade* (pronounced 'bad') commanded

14 *all confound* do away with entirely

15 *In feathered briefness* with winged speed

20 *your fancies' thankful doom* the gratifying decision of your imaginations (to co-operate)

3 No stage direction is given in Q. It is customary to provide an entry for the priestesses and Cerimon at the beginning of V.2, before Gower speaks, and an entry for Pericles' party at this later point. It is better to think of the Ephesians filing in towards the end of Gower's speech, followed immediately by Pericles and the others, to give effect to Gower's last four lines.

7   *Wears yet thy silver livery* is still a virgin

10 *Mytilene*. In spite of the scansion, this should still be pronounced with three syllables (see the note to IV.4.51).

11 *Riding* as we rode at anchor

13 *favour* appearance

18 *appearer* (someone who appears, comes into one's notice)

29–30 *If he be . . . no licentious ear* if this man proves not to be my husband, my holy office will stop me listening to the promptings of my womanhood. The meaning of this remark has been disputed. It was understood in the eighteenth century that *sense* had here its very common meaning of 'sensual inclination', and it has been left to the emancipated twentieth century to find this shocking, and to prefer to believe that the sense of sight is all that Thaisa refers to. But Thaisa, after fourteen years, responds to the sight of Pericles as a wife would. She knows, however, that the yearning she feels is for her husband, and not for a man who looks like her husband. If he turns out not to be Pericles, the instinct of her chastity will prevent her from a false affection. This is the married chastity which is partly the subject of the play.

37–9 *Now I know you better . . . such a ring*. Thaisa sees the ring on Pericles' finger.

38 *parted* departed from

40 *No more, you gods*. Pericles asks nothing more of life; his past sufferings are obliterated and he would be content to die at this moment.

41 *you shall do well* (continues his address to the gods)

48 *yielded* brought forth

61 *resolve you* clear up your difficulties

70 *night-oblations* evening prayers and devotions

73 *ornament* (his beard)

74 *Makes* which makes
    to form into shape

77   *credit* trustworthiness

83–4   *our longing stay | To hear the rest untold* delay our longing to hear what remains untold

Epilogue

12   *his cursèd deed.* Many editors understandably prefer to read 'their' for *his*, since Dionyza was the leading criminal.

13   *to rage the city turn* the citizens become enraged

15   *to consent.* Q reads 'so content', which is a difficult though not impossible reading. The present emendation, supposing a compositor's misreading, or an accidental transposition of 't' and 's', gives a much more plausible wording.

16   *although not done, but meant* although it was not put into practice but only intended

AN ACCOUNT OF THE TEXT

ON 20 May 1608 the publisher Edward Blount took two play-house manuscripts to Stationers' Hall in London, and had them entered in the Register, following the usual procedure for securing the copyright of works which it was intended to publish. One manuscript was of Shakespeare's *Antony and Cleopatra* and the second was *Pericles, Prince of Tyre*. As Blount never published either of these plays it is possible that he registered his copyright at the instigation of the actors, the King's Men, to prevent unauthorized publication by others. Blount took to Stationers' Hall the actual prompt-copy of *Pericles* used in the theatre, for it is referred to in the Register as 'the book of *Pericles, Prince of Tyre*', and 'the book' is the technical name for the prompt-copy.

If Blount's entry was a 'blocking' entry, it was not successful with *Pericles*. George Wilkins's prose narrative, *The Painful Adventures of Pericles, Prince of Tyre*, published in 1608 (possibly even before Blount's entry), is not strictly a piracy, though it claimed to be the 'true history of the play of *Pericles*' as it had been presented by the King's Men. But there cannot be much doubt that the quarto published in 1609 was a venture unauthorized by the actors. The publisher was Henry Gosson. It is conceivable (though unlikely) that Blount transferred his copyright in the play without registering the transfer, but the condition of the text is such that even if Gosson was in the clear with the Stationers' Company over the copyright he cannot have published his text with the approval of the theatre. Most probably, Gosson's book was not legitimate from either the publishing or the theatrical point of view.

Gosson's title-page carried a long legend: *The late and much admired play called Pericles, Prince of Tyre. With the true relation*

of the whole history, adventures, and fortunes of the said Prince:
as also the no less strange and worthy accidents in the birth and
life of his daughter Mariana. As it hath been divers and sundry
times acted by His Majesty's Servants, at the Globe on the Bank-
side. By William Shakespeare. It is not possible that the text of
the play as it is printed was by Shakespeare. Even in the more
obviously Shakespearian tone of the last three acts we have little
more than a long collection of Shakespearian phrases, somewhat
damaged, joined together with an inferior continuo. Shakespeare apart, the text cannot represent anything used in or
legally issuing from the theatre, whether it be the dramatist's
draft or fair copy, a scribe's transcript, or the prompt-book
itself. One outside possibility which may suggest itself ought to
be dismissed at once. Suppose the 'book' of the play which
Blount took to Stationers' Hall had been lost or destroyed, and
the King's Men had then decided to reconstruct the text, could
the result have been Gosson's Quarto? The answer must be no.
Shakespeare was still alive, and even if he was too busy or
unwilling to help in the restoration, the actors themselves would
with the assistance of their written parts have produced a text
which, even if not a perfect transcript, would have been free
from the major deficiencies in language and action shown in the
Quarto.

Although the evidence strongly suggests that the 1609 text of
Pericles is a serious misrepresentation of what was acted at the
Globe, it has to be said that as reconstructed texts go Gosson's
publication is a very serious attempt to produce a full text, and
enormous effort must have gone into it. It is by no means
impossible that someone associated with the play, perhaps a
minor actor, lent his assistance, or that surreptitious notes were
made from playhouse manuscripts. The evidence that the text *is*
deficient and corrupt is mostly internal, but some external
evidence is provided by Wilkins's prose narrative. The general
theory has already been advanced in the Introduction that two
'reporters' may have been engaged in assembling the text, the
first being responsible for the first two acts and the second for
the last three. The task of trying to infer from the appearance of

the printed text what the manuscripts presented to the printer looked like is made more complicated by the fact that the Quarto was set up in type by three compositors, whose idiosyncrasies have left their marks on the text. However, it is perceptible that the copy for the first two acts must have been neater not only in the handwriting but also in the setting out of the verse than the copy for the last three acts. After III.1, most of the verse in the Quarto is set out as prose, and must have been prose in the manuscript handed to the printer. The proposition is, then, that there were two kinds of manuscript copy, each from a different reporter or reconstructor of the text. The first, it is suggested, *rewrote* what he had available of the authentic text into a very humdrum pattern of blank verse and rhymed couplets, whereas the second reporter, with more of the general text available to him, was content to put down what he had got without attention to whether it fell into verse lines or not.

In dealing with the kinds of errors and confusions in Gosson's Quarto, it is therefore convenient to separate the first two acts from the last three. I have already described (on pages 35–6 of the Introduction) the type of rhymed couplets in the first two acts which must represent 'illicit' rewriting because errors have been made *before* the rhyme has been created. Confusion in the action is especially evident in I.2. The reporter's notes or memory must have been insufficient to make the scene coherent, and there is a particularly bad join in the words given to the Lords at I.2.34–6 in order to provide a sort of cue for a speech by Helicanus whose actual context the reporter did not know. Wilkins helps us to piece out the sequence which the reporter had lost. A third tell-tale sign of 'reporting' is repetition. A similar context tends to trigger the reproduction of words belonging elsewhere (see the Commentary to I.1.29 and 32 and II.1.24 for examples). Fourthly, there is the obvious nonsense of the first two acts. Though some of this may be attributed to the compositors in the printing-house, most of it must have stood in the manuscript, representing an incomprehension by the reporter of what was actually said. Attempting to restore these passages is very difficult work, because often the corruption seems too deep-seated for the kind of sense achieved by tinkering to have any relevance (see the Commentary to I.3.26–7, II.1.54–5 and 115–16, and II.2.27 for examples). Perhaps the most wearying feature of the reporting in Acts I and II is not so much the passages which have been garbled into nonsense as those which yield a kind of lunatic sense (see the Commentary to I.1.19, I.4.91, II.1.6, II.3.51 and 105, and II.5.22 for examples). The argument is sometimes put forward that bad writing of this kind is just bad writing, and that the text of the early acts all too faithfully gives us the inadequacies of a fifth-rate writer. But the accumulation of almost meaningless jog-trot lines gives to the whole of the first two acts a feebleness which it is quite ridiculous to imagine Shakespeare associating himself with; nor would actors bother to learn such stuff. It is true that we must not confuse corruption in a text with literary feebleness, but in the Quarto confusion and feebleness merge together; the author of the feebleness is quite clearly the man who gets things wrong.

The reporter's corruptions in the last three acts are in a way much clearer, because they appear as gaps or sudden deflations in a text of high quality. The imperfections in the verse patterns will be obvious everywhere in the number of short lines and over-long lines which an editor is forced to print, however hard he tries to find a verse pattern in the blocks of prose in the Quarto. It is quite clear that it is a mistake to try to carve the 'prose' into standardized blocks of ten-syllable lines; the present edition allows more irregular lines than will be found in other editions, in the belief that it is important not to break up what look like authentic rhythmic units in the interest of presenting an appearance of prosodic regularity. Even so, the 'regularizing' that appears in the present edition goes far beyond one's belief in its authenticity.

There are confusions in the action in the last three acts as in the first two. Examples are the openings of III.2 and V.1 and the duplication of Boult's advertising mission in Mytilene. A mannerism of the reporter is the use of weak 'fillers'. In the brothel scenes everyone keeps saying 'come', 'come your ways' to Marina, and there are constant interjections of 'faith', 'why', 'how's this?', and 'hold'. In verse scenes, people begin their speeches with an otiose 'Sir' (see V.1 for examples). The repetition in Pericles' interrogation of Marina of such phrases as 'What were thy friends?' carries little conviction (see also the lameness of V.1.164). Attention is called to what is considered to be reporter's muddle or repetition in the Commentary to IV.1.5–6, IV.3.46–8, IV.4.38–43, and V.1.53, 160, and 206–9.

What seems to be the most serious defect in the reporting of the second half of the play, the handling of the scene between Lysimachus and Marina in the brothel in IV.6, is dealt with at length in the Introduction, pages 21–6, and in the Commentary. There it is shown that the corruptions can be understood only in connexion with George Wilkins's narrative, to which we must now turn.

Wilkins's prose 'history' of the play of *Pericles* is a puzzling and inconsistent work. For quite extensive passages, the source is not a play at all, but Laurence Twine's translation of the Apollonius legend, from which Wilkins cheerfully copies. At times he follows the action as given in the Quarto, but at a distance; at times he presents perplexing alternatives to the Quarto version. Sometimes he confirms what is given in the Quarto almost word for word. Here is one such passage:

Quarto (III.1.30–33)

> Thou art the rudeliest welcome to this world
> That ever was prince's child. Happy what follows!
> Thou hast as chiding a nativity
> As fire, air, water, earth, and heaven can make. . . .

Wilkins (page 519)

. . . thou art as rudely welcome to the world as ever princess' babe was, and hast as chiding a nativity as fire, air, earth, and water can afford thee. . . .

And in a number of parallel passages, Wilkins gives us a word or phrase which is clearly more correct than the equivalent in the

Quarto; these are pointed out in the Commentary (for example at II.1.156 and III.3.29).

Sometimes, however, Wilkins's corrections are more profound. At III.2.82–5, for example, there is almost certainly a misunderstanding by the reporter, which Wilkins corrects. According to the Quarto, Cerimon has heard of an Egyptian who was recovered from death; according to Wilkins the Egyptian in question was the one who had the power to restore life (see the Commentary). At this point Wilkins seems to me so clearly more authentic that I have accommodated his version into the text of this edition. Other insertions from Wilkins which have been accepted are 'A straggling Theseus born we know not where' at II.5.82, and a three-line passage at II.5.54–6. I also insert Pericles' pitying address to his new-born daughter, 'Poor inch of nature!' (III.1.34). Editors have only very recently begun to experiment with introducing phrases from Wilkins into the text; the wider use of Wilkins in this edition is the logical extension of a welcome innovation.

Wilkins, if used with care, confirms what is apparent for other reasons, that the Quarto is a corrupt text, and at times with a vivid word or phrase he suggests the kind of loss to which we have to resign ourselves throughout the play. Some scholars have argued that Wilkins reports a version of the play earlier than the version reported in the Quarto. The theory is discussed in the Introduction (pages 23–5); I do not myself believe there were two versions, and the only place where the argument affects the points mentioned here is the Lysimachus–Marina encounter (which is dealt with in the same passage of the Introduction).

An editor of *Pericles* has the rather gloomy task of trying to make the most of a poor text which he can never hope to bring back to its pristine condition. Though he has a great deal more freedom in the matter of emendations than editors of better texts, he is working at too great a distance from his author really to value that freedom. In general, the policy of the present edition is that it is better to put up with the irregularity, even the nonsense, of the Quarto rather than tinker with a passage which has gone beyond repair and from which the original meaning cannot be guessed. Nevertheless, a great many emendations and alterations made by previous editors have been accepted into the text, with the hope of making the play more readable and occasionally moving a little nearer to the lost text of what was spoken on Shakespeare's stage in 1608.

COLLATIONS

Quotations from the Quarto are given in the original spelling, except that 'long s' (ʃ) is replaced by 's'.

1a

The following list gives the more important readings which have been adopted from previous editions, and those first appearing in this edition. The first reading quoted is always the reading of the present edition; to the right of the square bracket is printed the rejected reading of the 1609 Quarto.

THE CHARACTERS IN THE PLAY] *there is no list in* Q

I *Chorus*

	11	these] those
	39	many a] many of
I.1.	25	boundless] bondlesse
	57	ANTIOCHUS] *not in* Q
	60, 61	'sayed] sayd
	112	our] your
	114	cancel] counsell
	128	you're] you
	137	shun] shew
I.2.	3	Be my] By me
	25	ostent] stint
	30	am] once
	41	wind] sparke

I.2.   71 Where, as] Whereas
        83 me] *not in* Q
        84 fears] feare
        86 he doubt] he doo't
       122 we'll] will
I.3.   34 betaken] (*this edition*); be take
        35 Now my] (*this edition*); now
I.4.   13 force us] (*this edition*); *not in* Q
        39 two summers] too sauers
        58 thou] thee
        67 Hath] That
        77 fear] leaue

II *Chorus*

        12 speken] spoken
        19 forthy] for though
        22 Sends word] Sau'd one
        24 hid intent ... murder] hid in Tent ... murdred
            corrected to had intent ... murder
II.1.   12 What ho, Pilch!] What, to pelch?
        17 fetch thee] fetch'th
        48 finny] fenny
        78 quotha] ke-tha
        81 holidays] all day
        82 moreo'er] more; or
        90 your] you
        99 is] I
       122 thy] *not in* Q
       130 from] Fame
            may't] may
       156 rapture] rupture
       159 delightful] delight
II.2.   27 *dolcera che per forza*] (*this edition*); *doleera kee
            per forsa*
        30 *pompae*] *Pompey*
II.3.   2 To] I
        13 yours] your
        26 Envied] Enuies

II.3.   29   but] not
        34, 35   He has] ha's
          37   Yon] You
          38   me] *not in* Q
               what] (*this edition*); that
          43   son's] sonne
          50   stored] stur'd
          51   you do] do you
II.4.   10   Their] those
          22   welcome. Happy] welcome happy
          28   And] (*this edition*); Or
          34   indeed's] in deed
          35   this: kingdoms] this Kingdome is
          46   Further to bear] To forbeare
          56   endeavour it] endeauour

III *Chorus*

           6   'fore] from
           7   crickets] Cricket
           8   All] Are
          35   Y-ravishèd] Iranyshed
          46   fortune's mood] fortune mou'd
          60   sea-tossed] seas tost
III.1.   7   Thou storm, venomously] then storme venom-
               ously,
          11   midwife] my wife
          52   custom] easterne
          60   the ooze] oare
          62   And e'er-remaining] The ayre remayning
          65   paper] Taper
          67   coffer] Coffin
        73, 76   FIRST SAILOR] (*this edition*); 2
III.2.   0   two *Servants*] (*this edition*); *a seruant.*
          25   held] hold
          36   I] *not in* Q
          55   bitumed] bottomed
          64   too!] to
          92   breathes] breath

III.3.   29 Unscissored] vnsisterd
             hair] heyre
III.4.   6 bearing] learning
IV *Chorus*
         10 her] hie
             heart] art
         14 Seeks] Seeke
         17 ripe] right
             rite] sight
         21 she] they
         26 night-bird] night bed
         32 With dove] The Doue
             might the] might with the
         48 on] one
IV.1.   5 inflaming love in thy bosom] in flaming, thy loue
             bosome
         19 as] *not in* Q
         26 On the sea-margent] ere the sea marre it
         64 stem] sterne
IV.2.   4 much] much much
         71 like] *not in* Q
        101 Veroles] *Verollus*
        107 of] in
        121 BAWD] *Mari.*
IV.3.   6 A] O
         12 fact] face
      14–15 the Fates. | To foster is not] the fates to foster
             it, not
         27 prime] prince
         31 distain] disdaine
IV.4.   3 your] our
          7 scene] sceanes
          8 i'th'] with
         10 the] thy
         18 his] this
         19 grow on] grone
         29 puts] put

IV.4.	48	scene] Steare
IV.6.	35	dignifies] dignities
	65	it] *not in* Q
	83	aloof] aloft
	126	ways] way
	133	She] He
	184	I] *not in* Q
	193	women] woman

V Chorus

	8	silk, twin] Silke Twine
	13	lost] left
V.1.	31–2	any.| LYSIMACHUS Yet] any, yet
	33	HELICANUS] *Lys.*
	34	night] wight
	44	ports] parts
	47	with] *not in* Q
		is] *not in* Q
	64	presence] present
	68	I'd] I do
		wed] to wed
	71	feat] fate
	79	Marked] Marke
	101	countrywoman] Countrey women
	102	shores . . . shores] shewes . . . shewes
	121	palace] *Pallas*
	123	my] *not in* Q
	126	say] stay
	140	thou them?] thou
	154	as] *not in* Q
	162	dull] duld
	166	scorn to believe] scorne, beleeue
	207	and thou art] *not in* Q
	208	life] like
	214	thou art] th'art
	226	doubt] doat
	232	I hear] *ends the preceding speech of Lysimachus*
	245	life] like

V.1.	259	suit] sleight
V.3.	6	who] whom
	8	whom] who
	15	nun] mum
	22	one] in
	69	I] *not in* Q

Epilogue

	5	preserved] preferd
	12	to] *not in* Q
	15	to consent] (*this edition*); so content

1b

Passages from George Wilkins's prose version of the play of *Pericles* have been inserted into the text of this edition at the following points.

II.5.	54–6	That thus ... tender child
	82	A straggling ... where?
III.1.	34	Poor inch of nature!
III.2.	82–5	I have read ... health

2

The following list gives readings deriving from the 1609 Quarto which have been retained in this edition though many modern editions adopt alternative readings. The first reading quoted gives the Q reading as it appears in this edition. Rejected emendations are printed to the right of the square bracket, separated by a semi-colon where there is more than one.

I *Chorus*

	6	holidays] holy-ales
	21	peer] fere
	29	But] By
I.1.	8	embracements] the embracements

I.1.	129	untimely] uncomely
	130	pleasures] pleasure
I.2.	20	honour] honour him
	44	peace] a peace
	58	Do but you] Do you but
	66	you yourself] you
	100	grieve for them] grieve them
I.3.	26–7	King's seas] King's ears it
I.4.	17	helpers] helps
	69	me] men
II.1.	6	my] me
	32	devour] devours
	54	search] scratch it
	166	a goal] equal
II.2.	33	*Qui*] *Quod*
II.4.	32	give's] gives
	41	Try] For; By
III.1.	1	The] Thou
	26	Use] Vie
	75	for] from
III.2.	40	pleasure] treasure
	75	ever] even
III.3.	5	shakes] shafts; strokes
	6	haunt] hurt
	7	wonderingly] woundingly
	30	will] ill

IV *Chorus*

	47	carried] carry
IV.2.	19	there's two] they're too
	81	whip the gosling] whip thee, gosling
IV.3.	17	impious] pious
	28	courses] sources
IV.4.	24	true old] true-owed
IV.6.	23	iniquity have you,] iniquity, have you
V.1.	56	God] gods

Epilogue

| | 12 | his] their |

3

Stage directions
The stage directions of the original Quarto have been closely followed in this edition. The following list gives the more important additions and alterations. (The additions of un-controversial exits, asides, and indications of persons addressed have not been noted.) The first reading in the table refers to the present edition; to the right of the square bracket appears the reading of Q.

I.1.	64	*He reads aloud] not in Q*
	121	*Exeunt. Pericles remains alone] Manet Pericles solus.*
I.2.	1	*Exeunt Lords] not in Q*
	33	*Enter Helicanus and the Lords] Enter all the Lords to Pericles.*
	47	*He kneels] not in Q*
I.3.	28	*He comes forward] not in Q*
I.4.	98	*They kneel] not in Q*
II.1.	11	*He lies down] not in Q*
II.2.	0	*. . . with Lords and attendants . . .] . . . with atten-daunce . . .*
	16	*The First Knight . . . Thaisa] The first Knight passes by.*
	22	*The Second Knight passes by] The second Knight.*
	27	*The Third Knight passes by] 3. Knight.*
	30	*The Fourth Knight passes by] 4. Knight.*
	35	*The Fifth Knight passes by] 5. Knight.*
	38	*The Sixth Knight, Pericles, passes by] 6. Knight.*
	58	*Within] not in Q*
II.3.	0	*Enter Simonides . . . attendants] Enter the King and Knights from Tilting.*

III *Chorus*

	14	*Dumb show] not in Q*
		with Lychorida. The rest go out] not in Q

III.1.   14 *with a baby*] not in Q
          55 *She reveals the body of Thaisa*] not in Q
III.2.   0 *and two Servants*] *with a seruant.*
           4 *Exit Philemon*] not in Q
          10 *Exeunt Servants*] not in Q
          65 *He reads the scroll*] not in Q
          79 *Exit a servant*] not in Q
          88 *Music plays . . . Thaisa*] not in Q
          90 *Music again*] not in Q
IV.1.   50 *Exit Dionyza*] not in Q
          92 *He seizes her*] not in Q
          93 *Leonine runs away*] not in Q
          96 *Exeunt Pirates, carrying off Marina*] *Exit.*
IV.2.   52 *Exeunt Pander and Pirates*] not in Q
          87 *Enter Boult*] not in Q
IV.4.   0 *Enter Gower*] not in Q
          22 *Dumb show*] not in Q
             The rest go out] not in Q
IV.6.   36 *Exit Boult*] not in Q
          38 *Enter Boult with Marina*] not in Q
          41 *He gives her money*] not in Q
          61 *Exeunt Pander, Bawd, and Boult*] not in Q
         114 *Enter Boult*] not in Q
         118 *Exit*] not in Q
         128 *Enter Pander and Bawd*] *Enter Bawdes.*
         149 *Exeunt Pander and Bawd*] not in Q
V.1.   0 *one of Tyre and one of Mytilene*] not in Q
          10 *and Lords, with the Gentlemen*] not in Q
          32 *Helicanus draws a curtain revealing Pericles lying
             on a couch*] not in Q
          49 *Exit Lord*] not in Q
          62 *Enter Lord, with Marina and her companion*] not in
             Q
          78 *They withdraw*] not in Q
             Marina sings] *The Song.*
          79 *coming forward*] not in Q
          80 *withdrawing*] not in Q

82 *He pushes her away*] *not in* Q
234 *He sleeps*] *not in* Q
238 *Exeunt all but Pericles*] *not in* Q
Diana appears to Pericles in a vision] *Diana.*
248 *Exit*] *not in* Q
249 *waking*] *not in* Q
250 *Enter Helicanus, Lysimachus, and Marina*] *not in* Q
V.2. 0 *Enter Gower*] *not in* Q
V.3. 0 *Enter on one side . . . Lords*] *not in* Q
14 *She faints*] *not in* Q
45 *She kneels*] *not in* Q